ORLANDO

like a

By Rick Namey

Fodor's Travel Publications, Inc.
New York • Toronto • London • Sydney • Auckland
www.fodors.com

Orlando Like a Pro

EDITORS: Deborah Kaufman, Karen Cure
Editorial Contributors: Rita Aero, David Villanueva, Susan Blake, Howard and Donald Bradfute, Janet Tucker Butler, Ken Jones, Gail McKnight, Charles Namey, Ricky Namey, Terrie Namey, Tiffany Namey, Linda K. Schmidt, Donald Schutz
Editorial Production: Linda K. Schmidt
Maps: David Lindroth, *cartographer*; Bob Blake and Steven Amsterdam, *map editors*
Production/Manufacturing: Robert B. Shields
Creative Director: Fabrizio La Rocca
Text Design: Allison Saltzman
Cover Photograph: Kevin Kolczynski

Copyright

Special Sales

Fodor's Travel Publications are available at special discounts for bulk purchases for sales promotions or premiums. Special editions, including personalized covers, excerpts of existing guides, and corporate imprints, can be created in large quantities for special needs. For more information, contact your local bookseller or write to Special Markets, Fodor's Travel Publications, 201 East 50th Street, New York, NY 10022. Inquiries from Canada should be directed to your local Canadian bookseller or sent to Random House of Canada, Ltd., Marketing Department, 2775 Matheson Boulevard East, Mississauga, Ontario L4W 4P7. Inquiries from the United Kingdom should be sent to Fodor's Travel Publications, 20 Vauxhall Bridge Road, London SW1V 2SA, England.

Important Advice

You can use this book in the confidence that all prices and opening times are based on information supplied to us at press time; Fodor's cannot accept responsibility for any errors. Time inevitably brings changes, so always confirm information when it matters.

Acknowledgments

Robert Stricker, Rita Aero, Tom Schroder, Kevin Kolcynski, Glenn Haddad, Elias Fadool, Paul Meena, Lonnie Conte, Kalin Thomas Samuel, Jim Yeager, Charles Namey, John Sleasman, Bob Kaplus, Carol Biallas, Jim Canfield, David Milov, Jennifer Thielhelm, Jack Young, Kim Dawson, Tom Trevisani, Rhonda Murphy

Dedication

An extra special thank you to our family's favorite rock stars, the incredibly talented group "Sister Hazel," especially lead singer Ken Block, his wife, Tracy, and manager Andy Levine, and to the House of Blues' Stephanie Jones, for making a little boy feel very special at a very important time.

contents

CONTENTS

dear reader

Since childhood, I have believed that "when you wish upon a star, your dreams come true." Growing up in Baltimore, distant Disneyland was an impossible dream. So I simply wished the Magic Kingdom to come to me. My wish required the Russians to launch Sputnik, thereby necessitating the transfer of most of America's rocket engineers (including my father) to an unknown town in the middle of Florida. Then, in the mid-1960s, I asked my waterskiing buddy Craig Linton, whose dad was in real estate, "Hey Craig, why don't you get your dad to sell 30,000 acres of orange grove to Walt Disney to build a theme park so we could all go to it?" After graduating from college as a TV major, I didn't want to leave Orlando, while most of my graduating class went off to seek fame and fortune in New York and Los Angeles. I had no choice but to wish Universal Studios to me.

The rest is history.

Obviously, the person who originally wished the Disney and Universal parks all the way from California to Orlando is the person most qualified to show you around. You will also get three genuine natives at no additional charge: my wife, Terrie; 14-year-old Tiffany; and 11-year-old Ricky, who has not missed a single season at the theme parks in his entire life.

This is, and always has been, a family effort. Our goal is to help you and your family benefit from the knowledge that has taken us many years to acquire. We've tried our best to be accurate and complete (omitting only attractions we don't like and a lot of changeable details you can easily get elsewhere). Our wish is that our work makes your dreams come true.

–Rick Namey
Orlando, Florida

chapter 1

GRAB THE MOUSE
BY THE TAIL!

The average room rate in Central Florida is around $50. A soda in a Disney theme park costs around $2. If each person in a family of four has a soft drink with lunch and dinner and takes three cold-drink breaks—a reasonable proposition under the Florida sun—the group's daily cost for sodas will be $40. This comes close to the price of nightly lodging for many visiting families. And a full week of sodas costs the same as one discounted round-trip airplane ticket to Orlando from many major cities. Walt Disney World's press kit says that the Magic Kingdom serves more than 46 million Coca-Colas each year—and that's only Coca-Colas, and not any other beverages. That sounds to me like an enormous number of sodas. Yet in all the years I've been going to the theme parks, never once have I heard anyone say that the highlight of his or her vacation was the fabulous cola in the parks.

I'm not saying that you should go without cold drinks on hot days. I'm not picking on the cola guys. But as you read this book you will learn that I hate to be taken advantage of.

I wrote this book to help you avoid little things that rob you of your vacation dollars. I wrote this book to teach you things that only a person who's been here since they opened the place would know, to help you save money—and to show you how to save time. Because, ultimately, when you're on vacation, time is also money.

FIGURE THE HOURLY COST OF YOUR VACATION

Let me explain. To understand the real cost of your visit to each Central Florida attraction, you also have to prorate what you spent to get to the area and stay there. The corollary is that the real cost of riding, say, Space Mountain is not just the cost of getting into the Magic Kingdom. Riding Space Mountain also involves your transportation, lodging, meals, and multiday admission tickets during your entire trip. And you can prorate this figure to give you an idea of how much each waking hour you spend in Orlando actually costs. The hourly figure, together with my exclusive Worth-It Ratings, provide a great answer to the question that arises each time you start a new activity or step into a long line: "Is my experience going to be worth my time and my money?" My one- to five-star Worth-It Ratings reflect my opinion of whether the experience you'll have there is worth the money it will cost you to get it.

(You may notice that the ratings are generally high. That's because we've just left out attractions that aren't worth it—to spare you wasting time and money acquiring information about them.)

Here's how I figure the hourly cost.

Transportation: Start here. Figure the family's airfare, airport transportation at both ends, parking, and/or car rental. If you drive to Orlando, allow for fuel, lodging, and meals en route, and around 25 cents per mile for wear and tear on your car. Add the cost of transportation around Orlando, including bus fares or tour fees.

Food: Give yourself a daily budget that reflects meals you expect to have. In Orlando, a meal in a moderately priced restaurant might cost $20 to $30, excluding drinks, service, and tax; $30 to $40 in an expensive restaurant; and over $40 in a very expensive restaurant. In the theme parks, restaurants with table service are usually moderately priced. Fast food costs the same here as everywhere. To be perfectly accurate about your vacation costs, subtract your normal food budget for the period from your estimated vacation expenditure (after all, you'd have to eat anyway).

Lodging: Add the cost of your hotel. Be sure to include tax and allow for phone and incidentals.

Tickets and Souvenirs: You know about the tickets. The souvenirs are inevitable, too. To keep these costs down, give each family member an allowance over which he or she cannot go.

To get your estimated total vacation cost, add all these figures. Multiply the number of days you plan to be in Orlando by 12 (about how many hours most people tolerate in a theme park at a time). Then divide your total cost by total hours.

Let's look at how this works for the hypothetical Merlin family, New Yorkers staying eight days: Marvin, Mavis, 13-

FIGURE THE HOURLY COST OF YOUR VACATION

Walt Disney World

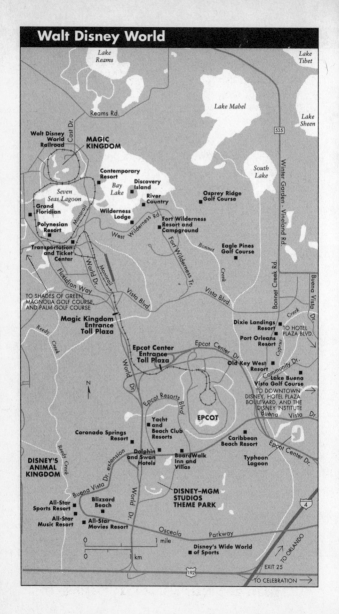

year-old Elizabeth, and 9-year-old Matthew. (Admission prices are without tax.)

The round-trip Newark–Orlando flight costs $230 per person, $920 for the family. In New Jersey, they spend $30 for airport transportation each way. In Orlando, they rent a mid-size car for a flat $150. Add $10 a day for gas for a total of $80.

They plan to eat mostly at inexpensive family restaurants, and they've allowed $960 for food, $560 more than they spend at home.

Lodging costs $52 a night. They budget $50 for movies and other incidentals at their hotel.

At Walt Disney World, they plan to visit the Magic Kingdom and Epcot. So they're buying two single-day, single-park Disney passes at $42 per day for each family member over 12 and $34 for Matthew. They get the seven-day Orlando FlexTicket to Universal Studios Escape, Sea World, and Wet 'n Wild for $159.95 each ($127.95 for Matthew). With one day left, they're heading for the Kennedy Space Center with the all-inclusive "Crew Pass" for $19 a head ($15 for Matthew). Each day, each person gets $10 in spending money; the family's total shopping allowance is $320.

Here's a recap of their budget:

Airfare and airport transport	$980
Rental car and gas	$230
Vacation food	$560
Hotel	$466
Magic Kingdom and Epcot passes	$320
Universal Studios Escape, Sea World, Wet 'n Wild passes	$607.80
Kennedy Space Center	$72
Shopping	$320
Total	$3,555.80

FIGURE THE HOURLY COST OF YOUR VACATION

At 12 hours per day, the Merlins have a total of 96 waking hours during their eight-day vacation. Dividing the $3,555.80 by 96 yields the hourly cost of the Merlins' vacation: $37.

Substitute your own figures. Then, when it looks like you're going to have to wait an hour to ride Dumbo, you won't just ask yourself if you want to take the time to ride. You'll also, inevitably, ask yourself whether you feel that a ride on Dumbo is *really* worth $37.

GO WHERE YOU WANT TO GO, DO WHAT YOU WANT TO DO!

Central Florida has no fewer than 15 theme parks. There are also seven water parks, over a dozen dinner shows, and several ticketed nightclub attractions. One of the reasons I wanted to write this book is that I've seen over and over that many people miss some of the best of them. When I was at Visitor Information Television and later at Visitor Information Radio, people constantly told us that the Kennedy Space Center was one of the top three places they wanted to visit. Yet surveys of what visitors actually saw always put the Kennedy Space Center below that. What happened? Why did so many people who wanted to go to the Space Center travel all the way to Central Florida, then miss it? Most of the locals I know agree with me that Universal Studios Escape is the best attraction in town. Although millions of people see it every year, millions still miss it. Why?

Part of the answer is probably the simple fact that after most families take in the Disney theme parks, they have neither time nor money left over. That's why I recommend an alternative strategy for your Central Florida vacation.

DO IT BACKWARDS Most people visit Disney first, and Disney does a really great job of taking advantage of that fact to keep them there—spending their money before they have a chance to spend it anywhere else. So by all means, figure out what you want to do in Orlando. And do it all. But if it includes destinations outside WDW, save the Mouse for last so that *you* see what *you* want.

I encourage you to begin your vacation at the park I consider the best in the world: Universal Studios Escape (around here we always call it "Universal" for short).

Universal is now positioning itself in direct competition with Walt Disney World. With the new CityWalk shopping and nightlife attraction and a second full-fledged theme park, Islands of Adventure—not to mention a resort with four new hotels and two golf courses—Universal is fast becoming a complete vacation destination.

MINIMIZE YOUR MOUSE We all know that Walt Disney World is the magnet that brings most people to Central Florida. However, some things at the parks are extremely expensive. And although some of them here (and at other theme parks) are not duplicated anywhere else in the world, many things are available elsewhere—and at a lower cost.

Outside Walt Disney World, for instance, you can buy enough stuff with pictures of Mickey, Donald, Goofy, and the other Disney characters to last you a lifetime. Ditto for food, supplies, and other necessities. And the prices for all this are significantly lower elsewhere.

Plus, Central Florida has a full complement of the national chains that save you money at home: Wal-Mart, KMart, Target, and others. There are also several chains of local discount outlets created to serve the attractions area.

When you need film, video tape, or sunscreen, don't buy it in the theme parks—Disney or otherwise. Visit a discount specialist. The Wal-Marts in the Disney area, among the world's largest, with food, pharmacy items, and liquor, are almost destination attractions!

GO WHEN YOU WANT TO GO Other guides make a lot of noise about the benefits of traveling off-season, when crowds are smaller and lines shorter. There are three problems with this theory.

First, it may not be possible to travel then. If your kids are in school, staying as long as you need to in order to see what you want means either missing school—or traveling when everyone else does.

Second, although lines may be shorter off-season, they may not move as quickly. Theme parks have the ability to open or close lines and add or subtract ride vehicles. This is not some conspiracy to cheat off-season guests. It's a way for parks to lower costs when there are fewer guests around.

Third, park hours are shorter off-season, so for any given length of vacation, the parks are available to you for fewer hours overall. Moreover, there may be fewer parades and shows. You may be paying less, but you're also getting less.

My advice? Go when you want to go. The basic experience varies little from season to season. Don't be afraid of peak times, because the parks are geared up to provide a peak experience. And don't stay away from off-peak times, either. Room and travel rates are lower, compensating for what you may be missing.

HOW TO SAVE MONEY ON LODGINGS

GET THE LOWEST RATE If you're looking for a low rate on a room, you could go from hotel to hotel or stop at a pay phone and check around. But you still wouldn't know where the lowest rates are. For the latest rates and information, try our own **Orlando Like A Pro** toll-free number and Web site (tel. 877/813–9390; www.likeapro.com).

Or try room brokers like **VacationWorks** (tel. 800/396–1883) or **Tamar Inns** (tel. 800/999–6327). There is a standing rule in the hotel business that says, "An unsold room night is gone forever." Therefore, anything that a hotel can get out of a room is better than nothing. Room brokers purchase blocks of room nights from hotels; typically, they either commit to a high number of room nights in advance, or they pick up leftover rooms on a daily basis. Either way, they get incredibly low rates and pass the savings on to you. So a family of four can pay as little as $23 a night with no extra-person charges in a decent chain property. Or up to six can stay in a two-bedroom suite with a kitchen for an incredible $49 a night at a major chain hotel in the attractions area.

AVOID PHONE-RATE RIPOFFS During my years in the tourist industry, many hotels have told me that phone charges are their number-one source of extra revenue. For instance, there was the very nice hotel on U.S. 192, a major thoroughfare, where I used to book business associates at an unbelievably low $32 a night. The catch was that the phone charges were outrageous. For business people who had to make a lot of calls, that $32 quickly became $100. When planning your trip to Orlando, be sure to consider your need for a telephone when you book your lodging. Remember that you'll probably be calling locally a lot, to make reservations and get information. Even local charges add up. And just because the hotel uses AT&T, Sprint, or MCI doesn't mean you're protected: Prices on calls for access to them can be horrendous. So can making credit-card calls from your room.

In advance, find out local and long-distance rates (including those you make with your calling card or via Sprint, AT&T, or MCI). Then negotiate a better deal. And get it in writing.

SAVE BIG ON TICKETS (OR GET THEM FREE)

It's a lot easier than you imagine to save a few bucks.

NEVER PAY FULL PRICE Don't buy theme-park tickets at the gate. That may be the worst possible place to buy them. Not only will you pay more—you'll have to wait in line to do it. You'll find little booths with signs inviting you to ask about free or discount attraction tickets at convenience and souvenir stores, in parking lots, and in hotel lobbies as far north as Pedro's South of the Border, a hotel and attraction complex near Dillon, South Carolina. These booths are known in the trade as OPCs, short for Off-Premises Contractors, and they sell tickets at between 10% and 20% off the walk-in price. For a family of four, the saving is about $20 a day—$100 for a five-day vacation! Plus, you'll also save time standing in line.

(By the way, children under 3 are usually admitted to theme parks free—though I wouldn't be surprised to see that change. I can still recall a time when the parks allowed children to stay "children" until the age of 12. Now the theme parks define "children" as people nine and under. I feel uncomfortable with that designation. I don't know about you, but I don't think of 10-year-olds as adults.)

NEGOTIATE WITH YOUR HOTEL FOR FREEBIES A travel agent may not get you the best deal on a hotel room, at least one in Orlando. For that, you have to deal with the hotel directly—preferably from home rather than while you're standing at the front desk, credit card in hand, with the kids just over your shoulder impatiently asking questions.

At chain hotels, which tend to have smaller staffs—Days Inns, Holiday Inns, and the like—ask for the manager, who is usually easily accessible. Say when you're coming and how long you plan to stay, and mention that you are comparing a number of properties to get the best deal. I usually say something like, "Sharpen your pencil, now. I'm going to be calling a lot of properties and comparing what they offer. If you want my business, I need your very best deal, now. Otherwise, if I get a better one down the street, you probably won't hear from me again." Actually, if they're at all competitive, they will probably hear from me again regardless, because—and this is my favorite part—I always call them back to tell them my best deal and let them bid against it. Believe me, if you don't use a wholesale broker, you have to shop the hotels this way. Even if you call a couple of places and take the rate they give you, you'll overpay.

When you negotiate, it helps to understand a little about the local hotel business. One of the yardsticks by which hotel owners measure their managers and staffs is by the hotel's "average room rate," an average of what's taken in for all the hotel's room nights per night, per season, and per year. You probably already know that air fares vary widely; you can sit next to someone who paid half as much or even twice as much as you did. That's also true of room rates. Because the management is so conscious of its average room rate, there is a rate beneath which they will not go. But the fact that your negotiations have brought you to this rate does not mean that the manager has nothing left to offer.

Many hotels have a stash of attraction tickets. Hotel employees often get them as personal gifts from the various theme parks, who hope to persuade staffers to recommend a visit. The more people they send, the more free tickets they get. Other tickets may have been purchased from the theme parks, often at a discount, to resell to guests at a profit. If a manager really needs the room night, he or she may part with a few tickets.

Although you will seldom find these so-called comps at $22-a-night motels along U.S. 192, there are exceptions—particularly if you promise to stay a week or longer. In general, the closer the attraction, the more likely a hotel is to have comps to give away. For free Disney tickets, your best chance is at hotels on-property in the Walt Disney World Village area and off-property in the Lake Buena Vista area. For Universal, the best odds are at motels on the north end of International Drive, another tourist main drag; for Sea World, next door to the park on the south end of I-Drive (as International Drive is known around town). And so on.

Go for comps for water park and dinner shows first. They're easier to get, though the normal prices are similar to those at theme parks. Basically, if you're going to pay for some of your tickets and get some free, it doesn't matter which are which.

Remember that the hotels get discounts, even on passes they buy. You should, too. So if you can't get comps (maybe because you got such a good deal on your room), try to buy tickets outright at a discount. Just say that you know that the hotel is selling tickets at a markup and that you want to buy tickets at the wholesale price as a condition of choosing that hotel.

If shuttle service to attractions is not included in your room rate, ask for a freebie when you negotiate over your room. Many hotels offer shuttles to attractions, and usually some passengers have paid and some haven't. Don't be one of the losers. Mears, the area's largest shuttle operator (tel. 407/423–5566), charges between $12 and $14 or more per person for one round trip between any given hotel and any given theme park. For a family of four, that would be as much as $56. A family's total outlay for lodging and transportation, when staying in a $40 room in a hotel without free shuttle service, would be comparable to the $96 they might pay for a room in a hotel that includes transportation. In other words, that $40 room is not the bargain they think. If you're not renting a car, a $74 room at the All-Star Resort, which is in Walt Disney World and includes all Disney transportation, actually leaves you with more money at the end of the day than a $30-a-night room on U.S. 192 that doesn't include any transportation.

Just because you're driving your own car doesn't mean the shuttle has no value to you. The hotel doesn't know that you have your own transportation. Transportation is worth something. When you're negotiating for your best rate, make sure that the hotel knows that you know this. Tell the manager that you've spoken with Mears and that you know the value of the transportation and are factoring that into the equation when comparing various room rates. All other things being equal, a room that doesn't include transportation should not sell for the same rate as one that does.

Always keep in mind that Orlando has more hotel rooms than any other single locality on the entire planet. Though rates are extremely low and supply is very high, local developers keep building more. Except for a few peak weeks of the year, there is tremendous competition for your business. The hotels need you a lot more than you need them. You have the power—use it! If a hotel, including any of those on my list, acts like they don't want your business, move on! There are plenty more who do.

TOUR A TIME SHARE AND SAVE! When you buy a time share, as so-called interval-ownership resorts are informally known, you buy partial ownership of a town house or apartment, which you are then allowed to use for a given length of time during the year, usually one week. Whereas full ownership of this apartment would normally go for, say, $50,000 to $100,000, each time-share purchaser, buying a 1/52 interest, may pay only $8,000 to $20,000. Consequently, the developer extracts a total of between $400,000 and $1,000,000 from the unit. Because there is so much profit to be made, time-share promoters are willing to offer valuable incentives to induce you to tour their properties.

Time-share resorts offer some of Orlando's best accommodations, with excellent facilities. So you may well *want* to tour a time share. But if you're really serious about saving money, there's another good reason to do so. Some big operators pay cash—sometimes $50 to $75 to people who agree to take a 90-minute tour. Most others offer free attraction tickets. There are enough different properties offering free attraction tickets that if you'll simply let the developers feed you breakfast and entertain you every morning, you could conceivably spend every day of your vacation at a theme park for free. (And because you get breakfast as well as the free tickets, you'll come out ahead, even given the hourly cost of your vacation as figured above.)

To find out about these, keep your eyes open for OPCs, described above, who contract with time-share resorts to deliver people who are willing to take the tours. If you ask about the free tickets (as opposed to discounted tickets), the OPC operator will tell you about time-share tours.

Know the Rules: A time-share tour can be a relatively painless way to get free tickets, providing you know the rules. Always remember that time-share promoters are required by law to abide by any offer they make. If the terms read "No purchase necessary," then you are under no obligation to buy anything.

Many developers give the OPCs budgets with which to buy tickets to give away as premiums—enough to give you tickets to a Disney park, Universal, or another major attraction. But because anything they don't spend is profit, they try to get away with giving you the least expensive premium possible. Insist on tickets to a major park. And walk away if you don't get them. If you settle for a vague promise like, "I'll see what I can do," chances are you'll end up with tickets to Ralph's Roach Ranch and the Ball of String Museum.

The invitation to tour the property, which the OPC gives you when you agree to take the tour, spells out the rules of the game. Always get the premium offer in writing. If the OPC offers you two free tickets to Universal, the invitation should say "two free tickets to Universal Studios Florida." The invitation also details the qualifications you must meet. Generally, you must be married and traveling with your spouse, have at least $40,000 annual household income, live outside Florida, and be "creditworthy."

Always Take the Morning Tour: This usually gets you free breakfast. It also interferes least with your day. Remember that by law the operator has to abide by his offer. If the offer mentions a 90-minute presentation, then 90 minutes are all you are obligated to give. When 90 minutes are up, you are free to go, and they must provide transportation.

Don't Leave Without Your Premium: When the tour ends, the salesperson completes and verifies your certificate. You then turn it in at the time share's redemption office and get your premium—in this case, your theme park tickets.

You may actually want to buy a time share. If that's the case, take my advice: Look for a property that has the facilities you want and good security. Go for a larger property. Smaller ones don't offer the extras, and it's the extras that affect how easy your property is to exchange. Most larger time shares belong to an international network of properties and you can probably exchange your week for a week at another resort in the group. The more you have, the more you have to trade. And the quality of the network's other properties has a significant impact on your property's resale value.

If you are considering a previously owned time share, which costs less than a new one, make sure that it comes with the exchange privilege; sometimes it's not transferable, so the resale is not the bargain it seems.

USE THE ORLANDO FLEXTICKET Remember, this guide is meant to help you find the best values. Single-day, single-park tickets to most major attractions are just over $42, not including tax. I recommend the Orlando FlexTicket, which offers substantial savings over the single-day single-park price of admissions to Universal Studios Escape, Sea World, and Wet 'n Wild. In fact, at $159.95 for seven days, not including tax, the cost per day is only $22.85, just over half the cost of single-day, single-park tickets.

DON'T PAY TO PARK-HOP! Disney heavily promotes the "park-hopping" feature (which allows you to visit more than one park on any given day) and suggests that there is an added value with this privilege, available only on multiday Hopper passes.

I disagree. In my experience, the park-hopper feature has practically no value. That's because getting into a theme park takes time (and remember, time is very closely related to money). Getting into a theme park requires parking your car, waiting for a tram, riding it to the entrance, waiting in line there, and then walking from the entrance past the shops and eateries to the attractions. Leaving is the same process in reverse. Traveling between parks means taking a tram, bus, boat, or shuttle, and more waiting. Only the Magic Kingdom and Epcot are really convenient to each other. (But not all that convenient. A couple of years ago, in the off season, I left the Disney–MGM Studios at 4:30 PM headed for Disney's Old Key West Resort, where my companion intended to freshen up before a 6:30 dinner in Pleasure Island. Although we moved as quickly as we could and spent only 15 minutes at the hotel, we were an hour late for dinner.)

I simply can't recommend that you waste perfectly good ride-and-attraction time on the leaving-and-arriving routine. So I advise you against park-hopping. And I certainly don't recommend that you pay extra to do it.

Disney also makes a big deal out of the fact that these park-hopping passes, which cost less per day than one-day, one-park tickets, are good forever. They are. However, by state law (which says a lot about Florida politics), theme-park passes can't be transferred or sold. So if you live far from Orlando and never get back, the extra days may turn out to be worthless to you—and you wouldn't even be able to give them to your friends.

So stick with flexible one-day, one-park tickets at Disney. This will also leave you free to take advantage of Central Florida tourism's best-ever deal, the $159.95 Orlando FlexTicket, which buys unlimited admissions to Universal Studios Florida and Islands of Adventure, Sea World, *and* Wet 'n Wild for seven days. This works out to be a great value at $22.85 a day—much less than the $42 most parks charge for single-day admission.

SAVE MONEY ON SHOPPING AND INCIDENTALS!

BYO DRINKS If you really want to save money, one excellent place to cut back is on sodas. It absolutely galls me to pay $2 for a cola when a juice box that's easy to tote in my backpack or stash in a locker costs between a quarter and fifty cents. (I'll tell you more about the great lockers below.) And, as I said, I have yet to run into a family who told me how great the soft drinks were in the theme parks.

BYO FOOD The more you feed yourself, the more you can save. Theme-park fast food for four costs between $20 and $30 per meal; packing sandwiches can trim $40 to $50 a day off your budget. And no one ever seems to mind when we brown-bag it.

USE SHOPPING PASSES If there's something you must have that's available only inside one of the Disney theme parks, don't pay another admission: You can get a complimentary, limited-time shopping pass, a really nice feature made for us locals. Go to Guest Relations, ask for a shopping pass, tell them what you want to buy, and pay for a one-day admission. If you convince them you don't have the time to go elsewhere, they'll give you about an hour. Return to Guest Relations within the specified time, show your purchases, and claim a refund.

DON'T WASTE TIME GETTING AROUND

LEAVE THE DRIVING TO SOMEONE ELSE Surprisingly, you can get just about anywhere, even to the Space Center, more easily and cheaply on a shuttle. Buses to WDW, whether run by Disney or not, get you closer to the parks' entrance turnstiles and get you in and out of the park area with a lot less hassle. The same is true at other parks. You'll really appreciate the convenience at the end of the day, when the last thing you want is to wait in another line just to get to your car.

ALWAYS KNOW WHERE YOU ARE GOING Get good directions (and a good map) at your hotel or the airport, and use them. Bad directions can waste your time or, worse, get you in trouble. The popular Church Street Station, for example, borders a part of town where you really don't want to get lost—trust me.

Central Florida directions can be very confusing. Interstate 4, which is marked east and west (because it's an east–west highway, running between Daytona and Tampa), actually runs north and south through Orlando. When you're thinking about I–4, just remember that east is actually north, and west is really south.

Don't make the mistake that many visitors do of confusing I–4 with the area's other "I," I-Drive, the nickname for International Drive. The main attractions strip in the Magic Kingdom area, U.S. 192, also goes by many names. In this book we use its impossibly long formal name, the Irlo Bronson Memorial Highway. It's also called Space Coast Parkway; in downtown Kissimmee, it's Vine Street. U.S. 441 is also known as Orange Blossom Trail. There's not much here unless you're into XXX, except for the huge Florida Mall, which is worth your while only if your hometown malls are few and basic. Don't go without dependable transportation, good directions, and plenty of gas.

BEAT THE LINES!

I once saw a comedian on the Tonight show who began his stand-up act with the lines, "I just got back from Orlando. I'd like to do my impression of a day at Disney World." Then, he walked up and down the stage in small square patterns, simulating the mazelike path of a line at a theme park. The audience howled, then applauded. Everyone recognized a shared and despised experience.

Believe it or not, the parks are full of shortcuts, short lines, off-peak times at attractions and restaurants, and many other opportunities to save time. Think like a football player and look for the openings. Keep your eyes peeled and keep reprioritizing your schedule. Yes, it's a good idea to have a plan. But keep yourself open to the timesaving opportunities that are always popping up. The minutes you save will add up to extra rides at the end of the day.

I'm not promising freedom from lines. Unfortunately,

they're part of the deal. I *can* promise that if you follow my advice, the lines you do wait in will be shorter and fewer.

PARK SMART As I've said before, just arriving at the theme parks offers several opportunities to wait in line; leaving, you do the whole thing in reverse. However, although arriving guests usually straggle in throughout the day, most visitors leave at closing time. That's when you find the worst lines at the monorails and parking-lot trams (at the Disney parks)— and everyone's tired. That's why I devised my system of parking at the Disney hotels.

For the Magic Kingdom: With my system here, I skip the lines to park, I skip the wait for the tram to the main gate, and I skip the lines waiting for Magic Kingdom transportation. It's even better at the end of the day.

As I approach the toll booth at the main entrance, I get into the lane farthest to the right. I pay the parking fee and continue to keep to the right. When I see signs pointing to the hotels, I go either to the Polynesian Village Resort or the Contemporary Resort Hotel.

From the Poly (that's what the insiders call it), I turn in at the first entrance, stay to the right, and go to the last lot. This puts me next to the walkway into the Magic Kingdom. Then, I just walk down the path to the Transportation and Ticket Center (a.k.a. the TTC). Sometimes, during peak seasons, in the entrance lane to the Polynesian's parking lot, an attendant asks to see my hotel ID. I answer that I'm having breakfast in the hotel. In over 20 years, at least 100 times, this system has failed only twice. The attendant who turned me back told me that only registered guests could park at the hotel. He told me that in order to have breakfast there I should park in the main lot and take the bus to the Poly from the TTC. This left me in exactly the same position that I would have been in had I not tried.

At the Contemporary, I park as close to Space Mountain as possible since the walkway from the hotel to the Magic Kingdom is nearby. On the occasions that I was challenged and didn't get through, I went into the hotel and up to the Grand Canyon Concourse to catch the monorail, which stops right in the hotel. It's almost never crowded and takes me right into the park.

To Epcot and Disney–MGM Studios: Our new route for these is to park at Disney's BoardWalk (just follow the Epcot Resorts signs to Epcot Resorts Boulevard) and take the boats directly to the parks. We haven't had any trouble; Disney seems to want to encourage people to visit BoardWalk, which is a really neat place. Parking is free and so is the boat.

Universal, Sea World, Busch Gardens: All three are currently offering something they call Preferred Parking. For $5 above the regular $5 parking fee at Sea World and Busch Gardens, you park right near the front gate. At Universal, for an extra $6, you get valet parking. This is a big worth-it when you arrive, but it's even more so at the end of the day.

ARRIVE LATE AND LEAVE LATE Most people take an unrealistic view of how long they'll spend in a park. During peak seasons, when hours are extended, they may arrive at 9 AM and expect to leave at midnight. Some visitors even attempt this endurance contest with children. Few make it. As a result, park crowds thin considerably around dark.

That's why I always advise my friends, no matter which of our Orlando theme parks they're visiting, to sleep in (or to attend a free time-share breakfast and pick up free theme-park tickets). Relaxed and rested, they'll arrive late. They'll start at the front of their chosen park, where lines have abated, and stay late enough to see the fireworks. Then they'll have the park practically to themselves, along with a few thousand other parkwise visitors.

Related to this is my advice to:

BE CONTRARY Most people are creatures of habit, engaging in predictable behavior at predictable times. In theme parks, most visitors arrive between 9 and 10 AM. They eat lunch between 11 AM and 1:30 PM. They have dinner between 4 and 7 PM. Waits for all rides are shorter around lunch—and there are almost no lines for food between 2 and 3 PM.

While in the theme parks, my advice is the same: Be contrary. If you arrive early, head first for the back of your destination park. Most people start at the front. If you arrive after the park has been open for at least an hour, start at the front.

And remember that you can save a couple of hours a day eating at off-peak times. My family usually has lunch at about 2 PM.

Decide which attractions you want to visit most and do them in REVERSE order. Most people have the same favorites. As the day goes on the most popular rides become less crowded. If you visit them in reverse order, you'll see more and spend less time standing in lines. Lines for some popular attractions almost never thin out, particularly when they're relatively new. Line up when your tour through the park brings you to them. Then bite the bullet and wait.

The parades and fireworks at the theme parks are spectacular. But remember, you can't do everything and life is full of trade-offs. Lines are shortest during the parades and fireworks (and, during parades, particularly at the rides and shows nearest the parade route). Parades are usually late in the day, in the afternoon and at night. Decide what's more important—to see the parade or to catch that major ride.

KEEP LEFT AND DON'T FOLLOW THE CROWD I am constantly amazed by the behavior of people in a crowd. Most people follow the crowd. Crowds usually flow to the right. People in a hurry pass on the left. Stay to the left and you will usually be in the shortest and fastest lines. Also, many attractions run two lines. Because people follow each other and because the crowd moves right, there is often no line at all on the left. It's a Catch-22—no one is in the left line because no one is in the left line to follow. I've seen park attendants walk way out into a long line and remind people that there is another line open. Even on peak days, I have often entered rides with no lines at all, just by walking up the left lane—while hundreds waited patiently on the right.

I remember once in the Magic Kingdom when the line at Big Thunder Mountain stretched all the way down the hill. Looking up at the entrance, I noticed that the left lane was open. My family and I ran up to it, all the way to the entrance, and walked right onto the ride. We entered ahead of hundreds of people who had waited 45 minutes or more, simply because we knew enough not to follow the crowd.

In the Magic Kingdom's Haunted Mansion, the line suddenly moves into a big open area that is a sort of a free-for-all, just before visitors get into the ride vehicles. These are on the right. So the crowd always pushes in that direction, leaving a large open space along the left wall. We walk through this space—right to the head of the line. It works every time.

Remember, in any area where ropes mark off different queues, a line that's closed will always be indicated by a chain across the opening. If you see no chain, walk on in!

DON'T LINE UP WHEN THERE'S NO LINE Many rides and shows have lobby areas or other collection spots where people are asked to wait. The expectation is that they'll wait in a sort of orderly mob. However, most visitors form a line—out of habit—leaving large open spaces empty. As a fast-track opportunist, you can move right in.

Look for the door and stand near it. If you can't see where it is (because often these doors are disguised), ask the attendants: They'll tell you cheerfully where you'll be going next.

BE PARKWISE There are times that you find unusually short lines at even the most popular rides. Be parkwise: Don't bypass a short line to stick to a schedule, thinking that a particular ride always has short lines and you can come back to it later. Finding a short line is like finding money on the sidewalk. It won't be there for long.

PRAY FOR RAIN A typical summer day in Orlando starts out cloudy and gets progressively more so until mid- to late afternoon, when it rains for an hour or two. These are ideal days to visit the theme parks. The cloudy weather scares many people away. Although some hardy souls brave the clouds, many more are flushed out by the rain. When the rain lets up, you may find the theme park practically to yourself.

So come prepared. Or buy a rain poncho with Mickey's picture on it (about $7.50) or a souvenir umbrella bearing the likeness of the Mickster, Woody Woodpecker, or Shamu. Since most lines are covered most of the time, find a long line you've been avoiding as soon as the rain starts. By the end of the ride, the shower may be over.

Also remember that Florida is the lightning capital of the world and an umbrella can be a lightning rod. Put it down before crossing wide-open spaces.

HAVE A GREAT TIME!

DRESS FOR THE WEATHER—AND FOR COMFORT Did you hear the one about the man who survived a fall from the Tower of Terror? He was wearing his light fall suit! Bad jokes notwithstanding, this is important. Always check the forecast before you leave for Orlando. Check again every day before you leave your hotel. And dress appropriately.

In winter, cold air masses from the north occasionally push southward, and temperatures drop. Thinking back on Christmases past, I can remember many in the 80s and many in the 30s or 40s. But once a cold front moves through, the weather instantly becomes tropical again. Many 40-degree days are followed by 80-degree days and vice versa. Sometimes cold nights follow warm days. Around Thanksgiving and between Christmas and New Year's, when the theme parks are open late, this is a consideration. Bring a jacket or even a change of clothes. Although a good dousing from one of the water rides is great when it's 90 degrees, it's nice to have warm clothes for when the temperature drops.

SHIP YOUR PURCHASES—DON'T CARRY THEM If you're staying at a theme-park hotel, one of your many perks as a guest is free delivery of theme-park purchases to your room. Request it when you pay. And whether or not you're staying on-property, you can have purchases shipped anywhere in the world directly from the park. You pay only for the shipping—the parks generally do not tack on an extra charge for this service.

USE THE LOCKERS All parks have them, and I can't stress enough how helpful they can be, especially when the weather obliges you to bring warm clothes. Putting your things in a convenient locked box inside the theme park can make your whole day better. Over the years, I have seen many thousands of miserable people slogging around in the afternoon heat loaded down with gear and purchases.

Although no one can guarantee the safety of your stuff, I myself have never had a problem in over 20 years. Security in the parks is good, particularly around the lockers. And the lockers are safer than the trunk of your car in the parking lot.

I use the locker for heavy, bulky things, like jackets, sweaters, and rain ponchos. You will want your cameras to record the day's events on film and video. But you will be miserable if you lug this equipment around all day. Use the locker (discreetly) to give yourself a break.

We also bring:

- A couple of towels to dry off with.
- Extra clothes, at least for your small fry. Getting splashed has always been part of the fun, and several parks now have fountains and other water features meant for playing in—kids invariably end up soaked.
- A change of socks. You'll be amazed how much a pair of dry socks can do for you after a rain on a hot, sweaty day.
- Frozen box drinks.
- Sandwiches and snacks.
- Extra film and video tape.

RIDE THE FRONT CAR While hundreds or thousands of visitors wait in line for a seat in one of the Disney monorails, my family and I are being personally escorted to the front of the train by a uniformed attendant to ride with the driver. I have overheard first-time visitors to Walt Disney World whisper

"Who are they?" or "They must be VIPs." There's a trick to this, and I can tell you what it is.

We ask.

That's it. That's all.

We just ask.

Disney's absolutely unadvertised policy is that anyone who asks can usually get a front seat. This is true on almost any ride—the monorail, Space Mountain, Big Thunder Mountain, Splash Mountain, Pirates of the Caribbean, even It's a Small World. You may have to wait until the next ride, or even the one after that, but if you want a front seat, they'll try to accommodate you. As for the monorail, the panorama you see through the Plexiglas bubble is spectacular. As often as we have done it (50 times or more), it's always a thrill.

USE SUNSCREEN This may seem obvious, but believe me, it's not. At the end of the day in the theme parks I see way too many sunburned noses. Remember that Florida sun will burn you even on overcast days and in winter. So put on your sunblock—preferably one with a sun protection factor of 15 or higher—before you leave your motel, and bring extra. If you're going to a water park, be sure your sunblock is water-proof and refresh it every few hours if you're in the water.

BRING MOSQUITO REPELLENT Lots of people never even imagine they'll need it in theme parks. I speak from experience. If you're planning on visiting Discovery Island, Fort Wilderness, or a water park with a lot of nature like River Country, you'll need mosquito repellent. And you may even need it in the parks on summer evenings.

PREPARE TO GET WET In many parks (and not only the water parks), at least part of the fun is getting wet. As I said above, you may want to bring a round of dry clothe out s for the family. And, because seeing your kids get wet makes for great pictures, I always bring a zip-closing bag to put over my camera. (I use a gallon-size bag over my video camera.) Then I shoot right through the plastic—a poor man's sports camera! If you're worried, leave your camera at home and bring one of those waterproof one-time FunSaver cameras.

BEAT THE HEAT The Florida sun can wear you down. Next to staying inside where it's air-conditioned, the best way to beat the heat is to get wet. Our family used to cool off by spritzing each other with a spray bottle filled with water; lately we've discovered a version with electric fan attached, known as a "Squeeze 'n Breeze" (around $18 in the parks and only $8 at Wal-Mart and KMart). We can also be seen sticking our heads under the stream of water in the drinking fountains. Now and then, I step into the restroom, soak my T-shirt in the sink, and put it back on. It works! I'm cool for hours. (The one drawback: Tiffany, my daughter, and Ricky, my son, don't think so.)

BE KIND TO YOUR KIDS All too frequently I overhear parents in the theme parks yelling at their children, even hitting them. Sometimes even the best children need a little discipline. That's not what I'm talking about. I'm talking about overbearing parents who are herding their children through the parks, determined to make them have a good time or else. Yes, there are ways to get through the parks faster, but don't overdo it! Don't try so hard to do so much that you miss the most important thing of all—a good time.

HAVE A GREAT TIME!

chapter 2

ADMISSION PRICES AND WHERE TO FIND OUT MORE

I f you're visiting Universal Studios Escape, Sea World, and Wet 'n Wild, don't forget about the 7-day multipark **Orlando FlexTicket** ($159.95, $127.95 for kids 3–9). A 10-day FlexTicket costs $196.95 ($157.95 for children 3–9) and also includes Busch Gardens. These prices and those below do not include tax. Before you hand over your credit card, ask about special AAA and senior-citizen rates.

BUSCH GARDENS Tickets cost $40.95 ($34.95 for children 3–9). A combined ticket to Busch Gardens and Sea World costs $79. Parking is $5 for cars ($10 for Preferred Parking; *see* Chapter 5), $6 for trucks and campers.
Hours: Daily 9:30–6, as late as 9 during peak periods.
More Information: Busch Gardens, Box 9158, Tampa 33674, tel. 813/987–5082.

SEA WORLD One-day tickets cost $42 ($34 for children 3–9). A combined ticket to Sea World and Busch Gardens costs $79. Parking is $5 for cars (Shamu's Preferred Parking $10), $7 for RVs and campers.

Hours: Daily 9–7, as late as 10 during peak periods

More Information: Sea World, 7007 Sea Harbor Dr., Orlando 32821, tel. 407/351–3600.

UNIVERSAL STUDIOS ESCAPE Tickets to Universal Studios Florida cost $42 ($34 children 3–9); at this writing, ticket prices for Islands of Adventure were not available. However, 2-day combination Islands of Adventure–Universal Studios Florida tickets cost $79.95 ($64.95 for children 3–9); three days cost $99.95 ($79.95 for children 3–9). Get them at Orlando/Orange County Convention and Visitors Bureau office at 8723 International Dr. and you'll save a couple of dollars per ticket. Parking is $6 for cars ($12 for valet parking), $7 for campers.

Hours: Daily 9–6, as late as 10 during peak periods.

More Information: Universal Studios Escape, 1000 Universal Studios Plaza, Orlando 32819-7610, tel. 407/363–8000.

WALT DISNEY WORLD Here we're talking about the major parks (**Magic Kingdom, Epcot, Disney–MGM Studios,** and **Disney's Animal Kingdom**), the water parks (**Typhoon Lagoon, Blizzard Beach,** and **River Country**), and **Discovery Island.** Single-day *tickets* admit you to one of the major parks at a time, *Hoppers* to more than one. Prices, which change regularly, are as follows, with prices for kids 3–9 in parentheses: one-day ticket $42 ($34); Five-Day Hopper $189 ($151); River Country $15.95 ($12.50); Discovery Island $11.95 ($6.50); combined River Country/Discovery Island $20.95

($15.50); Blizzard Beach and Typhoon Lagoon $25.95 ($20.50) each; Pleasure Island $17.95 for all visitors. Six- and seven-day passes are also available. *See* Chapter 1 for more on tickets and passes.

Tickets and passes can be ordered by mail (c/o Mail-Order Tickets, Walt Disney World, Box 10140, Lake Buena Vista, FL 32830); add $3 per order for postage and handling. Or they can be purchased at local Disney Stores, the theme parks, at on-site resorts (registered guests only), and at the WDW kiosk in Orlando International Airport. AAA offices nationwide sell discounted tickets.

To park in the theme parks you'll pay $5 ($6 for RVs and campers; free to Walt Disney World resort guests with ID and at Typhoon Lagoon, River Country, and Blizzard Beach). Save your receipt; if you visit another park on the same day, you won't have to pay twice to park.

Hours: Hours vary but are longest during peak periods, when the Magic Kingdom may stay open until midnight or later. Note that although the Magic Kingdom, Disney–MGM, and Epcot's Future World officially open at 9 (World Showcase at 11), visitors may enter the Magic Kingdom (Main Street Shopping only) at 8:30, even 8. Animal Kingdom is open Sun.–Thurs. 7–6, Fri. and Sat. 7–8. Discovery Island, River Country, Typhoon Lagoon, and Blizzard Beach operate daily 10–5 (during summer until 7 or occasionally 10).

More Information: For **general matters,** contact Guest Relations or Guest Services in any Disney theme park or hotel (tel. 407/824–4321). For **accommodations and shows,** call WDW Central Reservations (tel. 407/W–DISNEY). For information on Downtown Disney, call Guest Services (tel. 407/828–3058).

chapter 3

UNIVERSAL STUDIOS ESCAPE

From I–4, take Exit 29B. This exit is clearly marked "Universal."

 +

I have repeatedly called Universal Studios theme parks the best theme parks in the world. The rides are the most spectacular, the shows the most thrilling, the attention to detail unequaled anywhere. And now, with the opening of Universal's CityWalk, a dazzling new nightlife attraction, and the ultimate theme park, Universal's unbelievable new Islands of Adventure, Universal Studios Escape in Florida is the best vacation attraction in the world.

With typical panache, Universal has picked up the gauntlet to compete with Disney as a complete destination resort. Spending nearly $2 billion in the biggest expansion in theme-park history, they've purchased hundreds of acres of additional property along nearby Republic Drive and changed its name to Universal Boulevard. Plans call for multiple on-property hotels with golf courses and other amenities. To complete the experience, Universal has acquired nearby Wet 'n Wild, long the area's most popular water park.

Remember, the Universal complex isn't the product of some second-rate outfit. Universal is the studio that releases Steven Spielberg films, and it has a star-studded history. As good as WDW is, the Universal Studios Escape complex is shaping up to be even better.

Universal Studios Florida

Universal Studios Florida has long been my family's favorite park. Let me tell you why.

The Magic Kingdom is a wonderful park. It is very similar to Disneyland, the original theme park, which opened in 1956. It's full of neat things to see and do. But it's still based on many concepts from the 1950s.

Epcot Center is too much about shopping and eating and not enough about rides and shows.

The new Disney's Animal Kingdom Theme Park gave Disney a chance to push the envelope and boldly go where no park had gone before. Unfortunately, in my opinion, the Imagineers fell short of the task.

Disney–MGM Studios Theme Park remains the best of the Disney parks. And since it's movie-based, like Universal Studios Florida, comparisons between the two are easy. Both parks offer backlot tours that give you a behind-the-scenes look at how movies and TV shows are made. Both have first-class thrill rides and multimillion-dollar media productions.

In contrast to Disney's Star Tours, where your simulator is a small, square room and the screen is even smaller than those in your average mall multiplex cinema, Universal Studios' Back to the Future has you in an eight-passenger replica of a DeLorean sports car that literally hangs you out in space in front of a nine-story IMAX screen. Star Tours is great, but Back to the Future is a gazillion times more exciting.

The rides and shows are similar in structure at Universal Studios Florida and the WDW parks: there are simulators and thrill rides, special effects and stunt shows, interactive film shows and robotics (called Audio-Animatronics at Disney). However, in almost every case, Universal's version is bigger, more detailed, more powerfully presented, or just plain better. Although I have to give Disney the edge for cuteness and appeal to small children, Universal pleases the little ones with Barney and Baby Bop, Fievel's Playland, and my favorite kid's ride anywhere, the Funtastic World of Hanna-Barbera. But for all of us old enough to appreciate the pure power of motion-picture magic, sound, light, and spectacle, the winner is Universal Studios Florida.

WHAT'S NEW? Universal's original park just keeps on growing. This year's addition is the new Woody Woodpecker's KidZone, complete with a new kid-size roller coaster. ·

TIMING I recommend at least two days here—*before* you visit any of the Disney parks.

EATERTAINMENT Universal Studios has a bunch of decent munching stops that you may want to try for the experience or the convenience. There's a **character breakfast,** complete with Woody Woodpecker. (Bonus: Depending on how

Universal Studios

Funtastic World
of Hanna-
Barbera, **2**

Gory, Gruesome
&Grotesque
Horror
Make-Up
Show, **21**

Hercules &
Xena: Wizards of
the Screen, **4**

Jaws, **12**

Kongfrontation, **8**

Lucy: A
Tribute, **23**

Nickelodeon
Studios, **1**

Production
Center
Information, **24**

Stage 54, **5**

Terminator 2
3-D, **22**

Twister, **7**

Wild, Wild,
Wild West
Stunt Show, **13**

Woody
Woodpecker's
Kidzone, **15**

quickly you finish, you can get an early jump on park activities.) I list my other picks below. Reservations usually aren't necessary but if you have your heart set on a specific place, book ahead (up to 48 hours in advance).

SHOPPERTOONITIES Universal offers a number of unique shopping opportunities for related logo items.

SHOWS AND TAPINGS A schedule of shows is posted on a signboard near the entrance. You get a printed schedule when you buy your ticket. If you lose yours, you can replace it at Guest Relations. But it's better to call ahead to find out what will be shooting when and then schedule your day in the park accordingly. Also ask how long the shoot will take: Because it's hard to slip out early and because even a half-hour show can easily take half a day or more to make, a shoot can really cut into your theme-park time if you're not careful. If you do decide to go, remember: The early bird gets first shot at tickets. Depending on the show, you will have to grab a seat or a place in line early, and you will have to wait; bring refreshments. The number to call is 407/363–8000.

THE LAY OF THE LAND Universal Studios Florida is laid out like a Hollywood back lot around a central lagoon, with areas that simulate Hollywood and Beverly Hills, New York City, Chicago, New England, and San Francisco, plus an area called Expo Center. Production Central highlights the mechanics of show biz.

THE FAST TRACK Most visitors bear right when they come into the park. Do what other people don't: Bear left when you enter and proceed clockwise around the park. Do the shows first. Rides are most crowded in the mornings, then thin out dramatically by afternoon. Be sure to take your time as you stroll: One of our favorite family pastimes is to try to recognize buildings and what movie we saw them in. If you overlook the little things, you'll miss a lot.

PRODUCTION CENTRAL

NICKELODEON STUDIOS TOUR Nickelodeon is one of the highest-rated cable networks—not just by kids, but by everybody. The line to tour the studios forms at the Slime Geyser, the giant fountain that blasts green goo high into the Florida sky. Glassed-in catwalks above the soundstages give you a unique view of real TV shows in progress. Kids get to see how their favorite substances, gak and slime, are made, and may even get a taste! Game Lab, at the very end of the Nick tour, is like a fake game show with people in your tour group chosen to participate based on enthusiasm. The games are quintessential Nick—very physical and messy, ending with one lucky (?) kid getting slimed.
Worth-It Rating ★★★★★ Minus 1 if you're traveling without kids.

FUNTASTIC WORLD OF HANNA-BARBERA This is the best ride for little kids anywhere. I wish Disney would do Peter Pan as well. Bill and Joe (Hanna and Barbera) give you a quick look at computer animation. Then you enter a large simulator where you join Yogi Bear in a daring rescue of Elroy Jetson from the evil clutches of Dick Dastardly and his sniveling mutt, Muttley. The lines are often short.
Worth-It Rating ★★★★★

ALFRED HITCHCOCK—THE ART OF MAKING MOVIES I remember being scared to death in 1963, when Tippi Hedren was attacked in Alfred Hitchcock's *The Birds*. But that was long ago and for most of the X and Echo generations, this show may be dated. The effects are pretty neat, though: You may want to check your clothes for droppings.

Worth-It Rating ★★★

HERCULES AND XENA: WIZARDS OF THE SCREEN This attraction is based on the TV version with Kevin Sorba as Hercules and Lucy Lawless as Xena. Even for old TV pros like me, the demonstrations of cutting-edge special effects and digital animation are impressive. The scenario is that the production is way behind, and you have to help the cast and crew, in an interactive participation event that takes you from filming to sound effects and voice-overs. Along the way, things get completely out of hand—that's the fun part!

The Fast Track: Act up and you could get a part. Have a camera ready, just in case.

Worth-It Rating ★★★★★

STAGE 54 An inside look at the props, costumes, and special effects that go into the latest Universal TV or film production. At this writing, it's *Babe: Pig in the City*, but you'll probably see something different. I like this kind of attraction, but this one is tiny and underdone. Still, it's amusing.

Worth-It Rating ★★★

THE BONEYARD Many visitors completely miss this not-necessarily-final resting place of props and gadgets from films gone by. That tarnished metal hulk once had the title role in

Jaws and was as big a star as Richard Dreyfuss. Look at him now. Take a minute to stop and smell the rust.
Worth-It Rating ★★★★★

PRODUCTION CENTER, SOUNDSTAGE WALK-THROUGHS

One of the things I love about Universal Studios Florida is that it is a real, working, major motion picture studio. Although the entrance to the movie studios is heavily guarded, doors to one side of the actual soundstages open onto the park. There's always a chance that a movie star (like Sly or Arnold) or a director (like Spielberg) will walk out into the park. Plus, there's almost always a walk-through tour where you can see a real movie soundstage complete with the sets. Nowhere else do you get such an authentic experience of the way movies are made. A must-see for movie buffs.
Worth-It Rating ★★★★★

BITES At **Classic Monsters Café**, the highlights are the broccoli cheese soup and specialty pizzas. No reservations.

NEW YORK

TWISTER The stars of *Twister,* Helen Hunt and Bill Paxton, greet you in a short film that introduces the premise of the movie—two scientists chasing tornadoes across the country. This kicks off your journey into a fabulous soundstage demonstration. Set designers experiment with the equipment that creates the spectacular weather effects for *Twister* and the forthcoming *Twister II.* As so often happens in theme parks,

things spin out of control until you end up in the middle of an indoor tornado. The effects are all around you. Everyone always asks, will you see the flying cow? Yes, and expect to get wet! And don't worry about the line: Outside as you wait, you get misted so that you stay cool; once inside, the queue area is air-conditioned so you may not mind the wait.
Worth-It Rating ★★★★★

KONGFRONTATION New York City's transit system brings you face to face with Ol' Banana Breath himself! Don't miss the distinctive odor of bananas in the air.
The Fast Track: Beware of the line here—there's a lot more inside than you might guess. The best time we've found to do this ride is late in the day.
Worth-It Rating ★★★★★

THE BLUES BROTHERS IN CHICAGO BOUND This show takes place in the street, in front of a reproduction of Jake and Elwood's walk-up from the movie. These guys are better than Aykroyd and Belushi!
Worth-It Rating ★★★★★

BEETLEJUICE'S ROCK AND ROLL GRAVEYARD REVUE Rock and roll with the ungrateful dead in this loud, last-gasp blast from the passed. It takes place on an outdoor stage, with lots of bright and smoky pyrotechnics. Bring earplugs.
Worth-It Rating ★★★★

BITES Remember *The Godfather?* I have it memorized. Really, the whole movie. **Louie's Italian Restaurant**, a Little Italy–style establishment, wasn't in the movie, but it could've been. Great pizza. **Finnegan's Bar and Grill**, an Irish pub where Universal staffers hang out after work, serves British beers along with hearty fare like shepherd's pie. Draw me a Guinness! To reserve, call 407/363–8757.

BUYS **Doc's,** on Delancey Street, is where the Blues Brothers shop. You can outfit yourself in khaki and a pith helmet at **Safari Outfitters,** next to Kongfrontation. Or have your photo taken with the giant simian. **Second Hand Rose** is a bargain basement full of discounted clothing and souvenirs.

SAN FRANCISCO/AMITYVILLE

EARTHQUAKE—THE BIG ONE Charlton Heston narrates a behind-the-scenes look at how the special effects for this classic film were made. Then you ride a subway into an 8.3 quake, complete with spectacular effects involving explosions and a lot of water. You might get wet. Act loud and crazy at the beginning and you could get picked to be an extra.
Worth-It Rating ★★★★

JAWS You are greeted with the unmistakable smell of wharf, then board a tour boat for a routine cruise around Amityville's harbor when suddenly you are attacked by a terrifying shark. It took over four years for the Universal Studios engineers to get this thing to work (in tests, the mechanical sharks actually sank the boats). The delay was worth it.
The Fast Track: Before you line up, stop at a shop and get a plastic bag to hold anything you don't want to get wet.
Worth-It Rating ★★★★★

WILD, WILD, WILD WEST STUNT SHOW This is a nifty look at how those shoot-'em-ups and blow-'em-ups are made.

These daring stunt men are "real" men and almost as good as the stunt women. At Halloween, this becomes Bill & Ted's Excellent Halloween Adventure and Stunt Show—a show so great that even Disney folks visit.

The Fast Track: Bring earplugs, especially for little kids.

Worth-It Rating ★★★★

BITES The steaks and seafood at **Lombard's Landing** are excellent, and it's a great place to watch the stunt show. To reserve, call 407/224–6400. Outside on the pier, a stand serves clam chowder in a bread bowl. Yum! **Richter's Burger Company** offers giant burgers, grilled chicken, hot dogs, huge shakes, and the trademark—*cheesequake* dessert.

BUYS Check out the wood and leather items at lagoon's-edge **Bayfront Crafts. Quint's Nautical Treasures** sells *Jaws* merchandise. At **Salty's Sketches,** in Amityville, you can have a caricature drawn. Then there's **Shaiken's Souvenirs,** across from the Epicenter, where you can actually feel the ground shake while you're shopping for *Earthquake* stuff.

EXPO CENTER

BACK TO THE FUTURE: THE RIDE I rate Back to the Future one of the best theme-park rides in the world. One of the greatest thrills of my career was when I attended its star-studded opening and rode nine times in a row! I also talked to Douglas Trumbull, the renowned Hollywood special-effects wizard who designed this amazing ride, using the same simulator technology developed for NASA to replicate spaceflight conditions. The adventure begins in line as you are greeted by a research assistant from Doc Brown's Institute for Future Living. Pay close attention to the TV monitors—they're not up there just to help you pass the time. The presentation will bring you up to speed on your mission to capture Biff, with impressive detail. Check the halls for memorabilia from previous visitors such as Leonardo da Vinci.

Your simulator is a model DeLorean, similar to the car in the film trilogy (the actual vehicle is out front). Once you're buckled up, a garage door opens to reveal the fact that you are suspended several stories up in front of one of the largest theater screens in the world, 90 feet high!

The Fast Track: The very best seat in the house is the center car on level five. Go ahead and ask the attendant for it. (You may even get it.) Occasionally, you can fast-track the left lane, but don't count on it.

Worth-It Rating ★★★★★ +

WOODY WOODPECKER'S KIDZONE Behind the lagoon where a *Psycho* house once stood is a new all-kids attraction. Small fry can ride a pint-size thriller, Woody Woodpecker's Nuthouse Coaster, then cool off in the fountain at Curious George Goes to Town, a play area with tire swings, climbing ladders, and even a miniature city.

The Fast Track: This may be a good place to start your day, before lines get too long.

Worth-It Rating ★★★★★ Subtract 4 if your kids are over 10.

A DAY IN THE PARK WITH BARNEY Too quickly, kids grow up. Sadly, mine are beyond Barney. Yours may still want to meet the famous purple dinosaur, Baby Bop, and pals at this live outdoor sing-along, play-along show on a revolving stage. In the cool outdoor play area, kids make music by

touching glowing, singing rocks. Check your show schedule.
The Fast Track: Get there early to sit up front or your kids
may have trouble seeing.

Worth-It Rating ★★★★★ Subtract 4 if you're over 5.

ANIMAL ACTORS STAGE Meet Lassie, Mister Ed, and many
other four-legged stars. You won't believe that animals can do
what they do here until you see them do it, and then you may
still not believe. Like many of the Orlando theme-park experiences, this trained-animal show is the best of its kind.

Worth-It Rating ★★★★★

FIEVEL'S PLAYLAND Everyday household items are huge in
Fievel Mouskewitz's land of the little. This world-class kids'
playground has the obligatory ball pits and moon walks, but
its centerpiece is a water slide—wonderful on a hot day.
The Fast Track: Be here when the mid-afternoon heat peaks.

Worth-It Rating ★★★★★

E.T. ADVENTURE This ride gives you another excellent look
at how movies are made. The setting is a realistic re-creation
of a Hollywood set, a forest full of topless concrete trees,
filled with props from *E.T.* You ride the bike with E.T. and
see how many scenes and special effects were done.
The Fast Track: Long lines—and nothing to be done about
it; get there early.

Worth-It Rating ★★★★ Add 1 if you have small children
or don't like thrill rides.

AT&T AT THE MOVIES Fans of America's largest phone company will love this showcase of its role in films over the years.
What, you've never gone to a movie to see an AT&T phone?

Worth-It Rating ★★★ Subtract 2 if you think your phone bill is too high.

BITES The **International Food Bazaar** is just like the food court at the mall, only better, with Italian, Greek, and American (among others). I like the killer desserts!

BUYS Just outside Back to the Future: The Ride, you'll find **Back to the Future Gifts** and about a million different reproductions of the time-traveling DeLorean. Want to own the shower curtain from the most famous shower scene in history? Or take home a towel or ash tray from the Bates Motel? Stop by the **Bates Motel Gift Shop.** Then there's **E.T.'s Toy Closet and Photo Spot,** with hard and soft E.T. toys and a place where you can have your photo taken with the famous alien on a bike or in a toy-filled closet. **Fievel's Playland Kiosk** is your source for Fievel toys.

HOLLYWOOD

GORY, GRUESOME & GROTESQUE HORROR MAKE-UP SHOW This how-to demonstration on the making of Hollywood's grossest goo is only for the strong of stomach, liver, and intestines. In fact, you'll see all of the above entrails and then some at this festival of gore.
The Fast Track: Don't go at lunchtime.
Worth-It Rating ★★★★ Subtract 3 if you are easily nauseated.

TERMINATOR 2: 3D When I was growing up in the 1950s, 3D film promoters predicted that exhibitors of the future would proffer their wares in special theaters showing only 3D movies. So far that has happened only at the theme parks. All these shows are worth seeing, but along with Back to the Future, one of the best rides in the world, T2 is also part of Universal Studios Florida. I consider T2 the number-one theme-park show in the world and the most spectacular production anywhere.

At the beginning, you enter the headquarters of a fictitious CyberDyne Systems (frighteningly similar to a not-so-fictitious West Coast company), where the future is being programmed. You are shown a wonderfully satirical film depicting the amazing things that computers will soon be doing for you. Fans of the Terminator movies will already know what everyone else will soon understand: the machines are trying to take over the world. If Linda Hamilton can't stop them with the help of renegade Terminator robot Arnold Schwarzenegger, humanity is doomed. Along with a 3D movie featuring Arnold, Linda, and other stars from the films, there are giant robots, incredibly realistic 3D effects, fast-moving props, and live actors on motorcycles zooming in and out of the screen so that it's difficult to distinguish what's real and what's not. Audiences give this show a standing ovation. I went home and hugged my Apple computer.

The Fast Track: There are three opportunities to fast-track here. When you enter the building, the left lane may be open. Next, look for the place where the line changes to an assembly area; most people try to stay in line, so you can move ahead. Finally, in the holding lobby just before the theater, you can move directly to the area in front of the doors.

Try not to sit in the front row. It's too close, and you don't see as much on the sides and in the back.
Worth-It Rating ★★★★★ +

LUCY: A TRIBUTE Anywhere else, this often-overlooked tribute to Lucille Ball would be a stand-alone attraction. Now, thanks to *Nick at Nite,* a whole new generation loves Lucy.
Worth-It Rating ★★★★

PRODUCTION TOURS Productions are often in progress on Universal soundstages, so call ahead to request a schedule. You'll generally come in through the back-lot entrance, then ride the tram into the soundstage area and end up as a member of the audience for a national TV show like *WCW Wrestling* or *Country Music Showdown.* If you're lucky, you might just see a movie being filmed. Big stars work here all the time (I've personally seen Steven Spielberg, Steve Martin, Roy Scheider, Michael J. Fox, and a few others.
Worth-It Rating ★★★★★

BITES Schwab's Pharmacy recreates the soda fountain where 40s film star Lana Turner was discovered. You can discover overstuffed sandwiches and excellent old-fashioned fountain treats. Try the chocolate ice-cream soda. **Mel's Drive-In,** the scene of George Lucas's classic, *American Graffiti,* is just like you remember. In **Café La Bamba,** they speak Tex-Mex. Try the yucca (it's a vegetable) or the ribs (Ricky loves 'em).

BUYS In the **Brown Derby Hat Shop,** you'll find every kind of hat. **Bull's Gym & Sports Merchandise** is the place to get Universal sweats and active wear. **Cyber Image-T2 Merchandise** sells replicas of Arnold's zippered leather jacket and a special cut of the movie with some great scenes that were left out. The **Dark Room**, a film store, displays great black-and-white photos on the walls. The color film you can buy is strictly modern. So is the developing. Check out **XX Studios Styles.** You can make yourself feel like Hollywood royalty, if you have enough money for its pricey 30s and 40s fashion. In **Movietime Portrait and Celebrity News,** you can step into vintage outfits and get your photo on the cover of *Variety.* Need a plastic Oscar or a clap-board scene slate for your home videos? Stop at **Silver Screen Collectibles**, next to Alfred Hitchcock. In the **Universal Cartoon Store**, next to E.T., you'll find everything imaginable that relates to Universal cartoons. **Universal Studios Store,** the biggest store in the park, has items from all the other theme shops plus Nickelodeon merchandise. In **Williams of Hollywood Photo Studio,** you pose in period-style costumes. In the Boneyard, between New York and Hollywood, you'll find **Jurassic Park Merchandise:** paraphernalia boldly emblazoned with the logo of the world's most famous fictitious theme park.

THE SHOW AT THE END OF THE DAY

DYNAMITE NIGHTS STUNTACULAR Remember those great speed-boat chases on "Miami Vice"? They're performed nightly on the lagoon, right in the middle of the park, along with fireworks and lots of explosions.
Worth-It Rating ★★★★ +

Islands of Adventure

Universal has cornered the market on superlatives with this new attraction. Working with park creative consultant Steven Spielberg, Universal's Mark Woodbury and his design team have used cutting-edge technology to combine such disparate themes as Marvel Comics superheroes, Dr. Seuss, and Jurassic Park to produce the masterpiece among theme parks, the standard by which all other parks must now be judged. With more state-of-the-art thrill rides than anywhere else, no other theme park even comes close.

THE LAY OF THE LAND Islands of Adventure is laid out as several theme islands. The hub, **Port of Entry,** is an eclectic mixture of the classic buildings of the ancient world.

MARVEL SUPER HERO ISLAND

THE AMAZING ADVENTURES OF SPIDER-MAN The Statue of Liberty has disappeared, and it's up to you and Spider-Man to recover it. With a never-before-seen combination of live action, robotics, pyrotechnics, and 3D effects, this action ride earns my vote for the best theme-park ride anywhere. **Worth-It Rating ★★★★★ +**

INCREDIBLE HULK COASTER At night it glows green like its namesake. The ride starts by duplicating the thrust of a U.S. Airforce F-16 attack jet, going from zero to 40 mph in two seconds. An ensuing 100-foot-high inversion has you experiencing honest-to-goodness weightlessness and six more up-

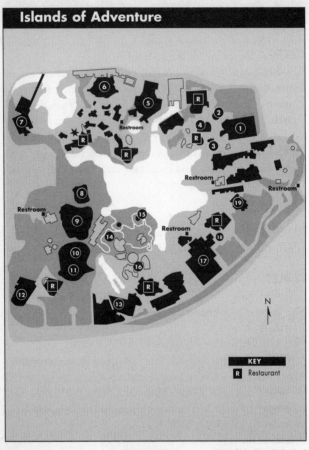

Islands of Adventure

KEY

R Restaurant

side-down rolls. And you'll plunge underground twice.
Worth-It Rating ★★★★★

DOCTOR DOOM'S FEARFALL This is UIOA's answer to Disney–MGM's Tower of Terror, but unlike TOT, which is indoors, this one is out in the open, so that you can see the ground coming straight at you in your terrifying free-fall.
Worth-It Rating ★★★★★

BITES **Captain America Diner** and **Fantastic Four Café** serve burgers and fries along with other classic American fare in a themed environment based on the Marvel Comics.

TOON LAGOON

DUDLEY DO-RIGHT'S RIPSAW FALLS Here you'll help save Nell from the evil Snidely Whiplash in the only flume ride ever to take you underwater.
Worth-It Rating ★★★★★

POPEYE AND BLUTO'S BILGE-RAT BARGES During this 16-feet-per-second white-water rafting adventure, other guests fire water cannons at you; the ride ends in a drive-through boat wash where there is absolutely no chance you won't get soaked—that is, if you aren't already.
Worth-It Rating ★★★★

POPEYE'S BOAT, THE OLIVE This is a nifty twist on the giant playground concept, with another water cannon in addition to the ropes, ladders, and slides.
Too new to rate.

COMIC STRIP LANE In this stroll-through area you'll see the habitat of Beetle Bailey, Blondie, Cathy, Hagar the Horrible, and many more funny-paper characters, over 80 in all.
Worth-It Rating ★★★★★

BITES In **Blondie's Deli,** Dagwood Bumstead's mile-high sandwiches are sold by the inch. Fans of Cathy know her vice is ice cream, so naturally, she's the star of **Cathy's Ice Cream. Wimpy's** immortalizes Popeye lovable sidekick.

JURASSIC PARK

JURASSIC PARK RIVER ADVENTURE Here the dinosaurs are the most realistic ever created. Among them is a five-story T-Rex that brushes against your vehicle just before you meet up with a torrential storm and plunge down an 85-foot water slide, the fastest and steepest ever built. The Hollywood park's version of Jurassic Park is fabulous, too—these are the best water coasters in any park.
Worth-It Rating ★★★★★

TRICERATOPS ENCOUNTER Meet a 24-foot-long, 10-foot-high robotic dinosaur, complete with facial tics.
Worth-It Rating ★★★★★

JURASSIC PARK DISCOVERY CENTER This faithful re-creation of the point of debarkation in the movie combines real fossilized dinosaurs with robotics such as the hatching of a baby raptor.
Worth-It Rating ★★★★

PTERANODON FLYERS The old skyride gets a facelift here—vehicles are prehistoric creatures with 10-foot wingspans.
Worth-It Rating ★★★★★

CAMP JURASSIC This is a new take on the Magic Kingdom's Tom Sawyer Island, with lava pits, caves, and a rain forest.
Worth-It Rating ★★★★★

BITES At **Thunder Falls Terrace,** set against the most literal backdrop imaginable—the 85-foot plunge at the Jurassic Park River Adventure—guests may view the victims' fates while chefs grill rotisserie chicken and ribs. **Pizza Predatoria** and **Hamburger Digs** are dino-themed.

LOST CONTINENT

POSEIDON'S FURY: ESCAPE FROM THE LOST CITY Another spectacular walk-through multimedia event puts you in the middle of a battle between Zeus, who is armed with 25-foot fire balls, and Poseidon, armed with a mere 350,000 gallons of water. You travel through the lost city of Atlantis, surrounded by a swirling whirlpool known as the Vortex. The show uses 180-degree projection screens and projections on cascading water to enact the battle between the two gods.
Worth-It Rating ★★★★★

DUELING DRAGONS Billed as the only ride of its kind in the world, this is the park's signature roller coaster. A single lift takes two coasters up 125 feet, then drops them down on two different tracks, where they avoid a head-on collision by a mere twelve inches. In all, you'll be upside down five times.
Worth-It Rating ★★★★★ +

EIGHTH VOYAGE OF SINDBAD One of the most ambitious stunt shows ever produced involves explosions in the water and amazing pyrotechnics, including a stunt person who falls 22 feet on fire.
Worth-It Rating ★★★★★

BITES Mythos Restaurant serves pan-fried crab cakes and lemon-pepper salmon with couscous, amid primeval special effects. The **Enchanted Oak** is based on the legend that Merlin was turned into a giant tree by an evil enchantress. The resulting structure houses a casual eatery that serves oak-fired barbecue, and the **Alchemy Bar,** which sells the park's own brew, Dragon Scale Ale.

SEUSS LANDING

It's about time somebody designed something truly cutting-edge for little ones.

CAT IN THE HAT: RIDE INSIDE Here six-passenger couches whirl through 18 amazing multidimensional adventures, with 130 effects, including a wallpaper-peeling tunnel and multiple appearances by that silly goldfish who tries to keep things under control.
Worth-It Rating ★★★★ +

ONE FISH, TWO FISH, RED FISH, BLUE FISH Remember this one? Here, if you listen to the rhyme carefully, you may be able to steer your two-passenger fish 15 feet up and down through the air, and pass the 18-foot squirt posts well enough to stay dry. Don't plan on it, though.

Worth-It Rating ★★★★ Add 1 if you have kids under 5.

CARO-SEUSS-EL You can control the action on this merry-go-round and clamber up on Seuss's most beloved characters: the cowfish from *McElligot's Pool,* the elephant birds from *Horton Hears a Who,* the aqua mop-tops and twin camels from *One Fish, Two Fish,* the dog-a-lopes and mulligatawnies from *If I Ran the Zoo,* and the birthday katroo from *Happy Birthday to You.*

Worth-It Rating ★★★★ Add 1 if you have kids under 5.

IF I RAN THE ZOO Similar to Fievel's Playland (*see above*), this lively playground is loaded with water effects—and there are 19 different play stations.

Worth-It Rating ★★★★★

BITES **Green Eggs and Ham Café** brings to life the Dr. Seuss classic with finely ground parsley adding the all-natural coloring to the signature dish, served (along with more traditional fare) in this park's premier character dining experience. At **Circus McGurkus Café Stoo-Pendous**, guests dine on classic American food while watching trapeze artists and jugglers. Stop for a quick ice cream or fruit juice at **Hop on Pop Ice Cream Shop** and **Moose Juice Goose Juice**, respectively.

chapter 4

SEA WORLD

*Take I–4. Use Exit 27A, "Sea World," eastbound; Exit 28, Route 528,
the Beeline Expressway, westbound. The park can also be easily
reached directly from the south end of International Drive
and from the I-Drive exit on the westbound Beeline.*

It's the best animal park in Orlando.

Sea World is a wonderful educational experience, and kids learn without being lectured. Knowledgeable staffers are on hand at every attraction to share their knowledge and answer questions. On our last visit a guide gave us a personal hour-long presentation on everything we'd ever wanted to know about polar bears. I am constantly amazed at the level of perception shown by even the smallest children here.

Moreover, attractions such as Sea World and Busch Gardens—both owned and operated by Anheuser-Busch—provide funding and expertise to protect many endangered animals. Every year Sea World staff respond to hundreds of calls for help, including many from state and federal authorities in need of an aquatic rescue.

WHAT'S NEW? You'll enter through a brand-new entrance modeled after a picturesque New England seaside village. Two eateries, both near the main entrance, are worth noting. The recently remodeled Cypress Bakery serves enormous treats like the giant, gooey, iced cinnamon roll I had for breakfast. Sweet Sailin' Confections is a candy shop for the serious chocoholic.

TIMING Stay as long as you can—from opening to closing off-season and around 12 hours when Sea World stays open late. (You *could* stay 15 hours, but that's too long for anyone to spend in a theme park, even Sea World.) Because of how shows are timed, it's nearly impossible to see them all. If you do, you'll have no time left for exhibits. So set your priorities based on what interests *you*—there are no bad shows at Sea World.

THE LAY OF THE LAND Sea World attractions, exhibits, and shows are arranged around a small lagoon.

THE FAST TRACK Except at the Wild Arctic, Sea World has few lines. Most people go to the right when they get here. My family goes the other direction, and I advise you to do the same. Here are some other tips:

- If you begin early, start in the back of the park and work forward. If you arrive late, start at the front. You'll get the best seats and views at shows.
- Near the entrance, pick up a computer printout with the day's shows; based on when you arrive, this recommends what to see. Plan your day around them.
- The bridge across the lake at Sea World's center is long and open. Because Florida lightning can be dan-

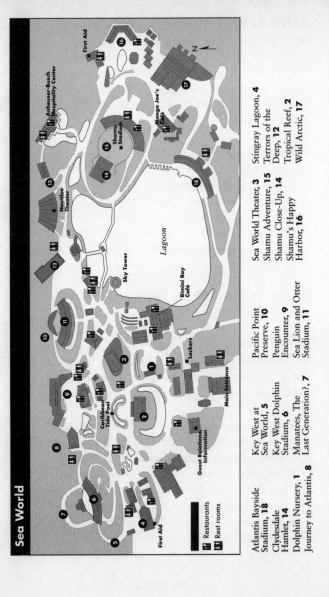

Sea World

First Aid

Anheuser-Busch
Hospitality Center

First Aid

Shamu
Stadium

Mango Joe's
Café

N

Nautilus
Theater

Lagoon

Sky Tower

Bimini Bay
Café

Lockers

Caribbean
Tide Pool

Guest Relations,
Information

Main Entrance

First Aid

■ Restaurants
鹵 Rest rooms

Atlantis Bayside
Stadium, **18**
Clydesdale
Hamlet, **14**
Dolphin Nursery, **1**
Journey to Atlantis, **8**

Key West at
Sea World, **5**
Key West Dolphin
Stadium, **6**
Manatees, The
Last Generation?, **7**

Pacific Point
Preserve, **10**
Penguin
Encounter, **9**
Sea Lion and Otter
Stadium, **11**

Sea World Theater, **3**
Shamu Adventure, **15**
Shamu Close-Up, **14**
Shamu's Happy
Harbor, **16**

Stingray Lagoon, **4**
Terrors of the
Deep, **12**
Tropical Reef, **2**
Wild Arctic, **17**

gerous, people sometimes stampede when a storm threatens. Watch out—and if it looks like rain, stay off the bridge.

- Consider a behind-the-scenes tour. The **Polar Expedition** takes you to meet polar bears, penguins, and beluga whales; the **Shark Tour** lets you feed and touch the ocean's most feared creatures. Cost is $9.95 per adult, $5.95 per child 3 and up. Reservations are neither required nor available, but it's best to sign up as early as you can; stop at the service desk on your left immediately after you enter the park.

- Sign up for Camp SeaWorld. SeaWorld's Education Department offers sleepover programs and courses for families. "SeaWorld Adventure Camps" are for teens interested in a career in the biological sciences. For information or reservations, call 407/363–2380.

WHAT TO SEA

TROPICAL REEF A cool refuge on a hot day, this giant aquarium would be a stand-alone attraction anywhere but Orlando. Little signs identify thousands of species, most from the Caribbean.
Worth-It Rating ★★★

SEA WORLD THEATER "Pets on Stage" is a live-action, performing animal show similar to Animal Actors at Universal.
Worth-It Rating ★★★★★

DOLPHIN NURSERY Newborn baby Flippers and their moms splash around in this nursery. My kids love it.
Worth-It Rating ★★★★

CARIBBEAN TIDE POOL Grab a surface scope (like a dive mask that you hold against the surface of the water to look through). You can see sea urchins, starfish, and anemones, and even handle them. A Sea World staffer hovers nearby and helps the kids ask the right questions. Cool pool!
Worth-It Rating ★★★★ Add 1 if you have kids.

WHALE AND DOLPHIN SHOW Trained humans run around the enormous Key West Dolphin Stadium and fetch fish for the highly intelligent sea mammals performing the breathtaking leaps of a graceful, intricate water ballet. Hundreds of whale hours have gone into teaching these two-legged land mammals to perform their tricks.
The Fast Track: One lucky child is picked to be in the show. Get there extra early and beg, and it might be yours.
Worth-It Rating ★★★★★

DOLPHIN INTERACTIVE PROGRAM For this two-hour education-and-participation program in the Key West Dolphin Stadium you actually get into the water with the trainer and the dolphins, and get to pet, feed, and hug your very own dolphin pal. Easily worth the extra cost ($159 for participants 13 and up, $55 for observers). It's available at 7 AM daily and sometimes at 10:30 AM.
The Fast Track: In peak season, this books up months in advance. If you want to DIP, find out what's available and schedule your vacation around it.
Worth-It Rating ★★★★★ +

MANATEES: THE LAST GENERATION? Thanks to legislation championed by the folks here and by Florida's own Jimmy Buffett, these gentle sea cows are making a comeback. In this nifty environment, you can view them above the water and beneath it, peacefully coexisting with some jumbo gators.
Worth-It Rating ★★★★★

KEY WEST AT SEA WORLD In this charming re-creation of Ernest Hemingway's Key West, you can have stingrays eating right out of your hand; learn the differences between porpoises and our home-grown Atlantic bottle-nosed dolphins; and, at designated times, buy smelts and toss them into the pool—smelly but fun.
Worth-It Rating ★★★★★

CLYDE AND SEAMORE TAKE PIRATE ISLAND This show in the Sea Lion and Otter Stadium stars the Laurel and Hardy of the water, Clyde Otter and Seamore Sea Lion. The new set, a spectacular pirate ship with tall masts and multilevel decks, gives these slippery characters plenty of space for sliding and gliding.
The Fast Track: There are lots of obstructions. You'll miss some of the best gags if you're too close to the stage or too far to either side. Go for the middle, halfway back.
Worth-It Rating ★★★★★

PACIFIC POINT PRESERVE This man-made tidal pool is complete with the rocky Pacific coast and rolling waves. Here, you'll learn the differences between sea lions and seals, and get the chance to throw 'em a fish! (The fish is on you.)
Worth-It Rating ★★★★ Add 1 if the cost of fish is not a factor.

PENGUIN ENCOUNTER Pop quiz! How do you tell a penguin from a puffin? Hint: There are no penguins at the North Pole. Both are here, in icy splendor. They're fast, they're funny, and they're all dressed up in black tie and tails.
Worth-It Rating ★★★★★

JOURNEY TO ATLANTIS This is the first of a new generation of rides called water coasters. Not flumes, these are more like giant roller coasters where you get wet. This one has two 60-foot drops. Special effects en route tell the tale of your mission: to warn the inhabitants of Atlantis about a terrible storm that threatens to submerge the entire continent.
The Fast Track: The only drawback is the long, hot line, with no water (even though it's a water ride—go figure) so be sure to bring your Squeeze 'n Breeze.
Worth-It Rating ★★★★★

TERRORS OF THE DEEP Don't miss this one! Live sharks circle right in front of you in an enormous tank. But wait, there's more! Step onto a moving sidewalk and you are slowly propelled through an enormous Plexiglas tube right through the middle of the shark tank!
Worth-It Rating ★★★★★

CLYDESDALE HAMLET Home of the world-famous Budweiser Clydesdales, the pride of Anheuser-Busch.
Worth-It Rating ★★★

SHAMU ADVENTURE If you guessed that Shamu Stadium is the home of Shamu, you're right. Themes change, so the show may well be called something else by the time you visit, but so what? You see the big guy on a big screen and in person with baby Shamu, too! Shamu is huge, jumps a lot, and lands with a thud (just like a few professional basketball players who get paid $20 million a year). At night, the show is "Shamu Rocks America." It's a lot like the day show, only at night with fireworks and rock music. Personally, I like Shamu best under the lights.

Worth-It Rating ★★★★★

SHAMU CLOSE-UP Here's your chance to see Shamu's family up close and personal in the world's largest fish bowl (okay, mammal bowl).

Worth-It Rating ★★★★★

SHAMU'S HAPPY HARBOR Imagine one of those McDonald's play places that's five stories high! This awesome playground is complete with a giant pirate ship and water cannons. Grown-ups can go, too—when accompanied by a child. And there's no waiting. Get wet, cool off—we do!

Worth-It Rating ★★★★★

WILD ARCTIC First, you take a simulator trip through the Arctic. Then you go through the world's largest walk-in freezer to view polar bears and other Arctic animals. The finale? A high-tech educational area to answer all your questions

Worth-It Rating ★★★★★

ATLANTIS BAYSIDE STADIUM Two teams compete at stunts and races in the current production, the "Intensity Water Ski Show." After dark? There must be a law that says that every theme park must have a fireworks show. "Red, White, and Blue Fireworks Spectacular," in the water-ski stadium after dark during peak season, is currently the town's biggest. Sea

World claims it's the biggest in the world! I've heard this claim so many times before that I'm skeptical, but this is certainly among the biggest.
Worth-It Rating ★★★★★

ANHEUSER-BUSCH HOSPITALITY CENTER Free beer! (Or you could stop here for sandwiches and snacks.) Check out the flamingos out front.
Worth-It Rating ★★★★★

EATERTAINMENT

The big deal is the **Luau,** a Polynesian dinner show (*see* Chapter 12). At the **Spinnaker Sidewalk Cafe,** we get clam chowder in a bread bowl, a family favorite. At the **Polar Parlor,** also near the entrance, the specialty is the giant waffle cone. The **Cypress Bakery,** near the front gate, serves up fresh-baked goodies—arrive early and do breakfast. **Bimini Bay Cafe,** next to the Luau, serves mostly sandwiches and burgers but also has a good island-style chowder. **Buccaneer Smokehouse,** in front of the Sea World Theater, and **Dockside Smokehouse,** next to Terrors of the Deep, are barbecue specialists. **Mama Stella's Italian Kitchen,** across from Penguin Encounter, serves pizza and pasta. At **Chicken 'n' Biscuit,** between the Sea World Theater and the Sea Lion and Otter Stadium, I love the double-chocolate cherry cake. Sandwiches are the fare at **Waterfront Sandwich Grill,** next to the Sea Lion and Otter Stadium, and the **Deli,** in the Anheuser-Busch Hospitality Center. At **Mango Joe's Cafe,** the sizzling fajitas are a great deal, and the seafood salad is wonderful.

SHOPPERTOONITIES

For aquatic mementos, Sea World is the place. **Shamu's Emporium, Shamu Souvenirs, Crosswalk, Outrigger, Sand Castle Toys 'n' Treats, Coconut Bay Trader,** and **Stadium Gifts** all stock a bit of everything, many items bearing pictures of Shamu. Check out **Discovery Cove** for educational toys; **Ocean Treasures, Pearl Factory,** and **Wild Arctic** for sea stuff. At **Cruz Kay Harbor,** you'll find that Hawaiian-print whatever you've been wanting (and not necessarily needing). **Flamingo Point** has hats and T-shirts. Bunches of people buy Anheuser-Busch logo souvenirs at the **Label Stable, Gulf Breeze Trader,** and **Gangway Gift Shop.** We love the frogs. Personalized souvenirs? **Kaman's Photo, Key Hole Photo,** and **Amazing Pictures** do novelty photos. You can have your face sketched at **Kaman's Artist** or painted at **Enjoy Your Face.** The Ringcutter, Pearl Factory, Your Name in Gold, and **Brewster Glassmith** make jewelry by hand. **Sand Art, First Names First,** and **Rainbow Art** also do custom items.

chapter 5

BUSCH GARDENS

*Take I–4 west to Tampa, then I–75 north to Busch Boulevard or fol-
low the signs. The park is about an hour and a half from Orlando.*

★★★★

Add 1 if you love animals or roller coasters.

*It's a great park and a great deal, especially if you use the Orlando
FlexTicket. One of my family's favorite parks.*

I n this 335-acre park from the brewers of the King of
Beers, the theme is a trip across Africa, and each area is
based on a different country; the park's ubiquitous German motifs are reminders of the Germans' colonization
of the continent (and the German heritage of Busch beer).
The roller-coaster and thrill-ride selection is second only to
the one at Universal's Islands of Adventure and is well worth
doing for true thrill-ride fans. Busch Gardens is known for
its world-ranked, hang-you-upside-down roller coasters.
They're the modern kind, with tubular steel tracks, different
from the sometimes larger rides with tracks built on wooden
scaffolding; the thrills come not from climbs and falls but
from speeding through tight turns and hanging upside
down.

But the rides are only part of the show. Surrounding the
part of the park devoted to rides, shows, and exhibits is a

huge botanical garden and zoological park, one of the world's first to abandon cages in favor of habitats. So take your time and be aware of your surroundings as you move from place to place.

WHICH ANIMAL KINGDOM? Busch Gardens, the original animal park, is still, by far, the best. Disney is planning a major expansion, adding Asia to its Animal Kingdom. When they do, things between the two parks may become competitive. At this writing, my recommendation for the best animal adventure-park experience is still Busch Gardens.

WHAT'S NEW? Gwazi, made up of twin 7,000-foot "dueling" wooden roller coasters, continues Busch Gardens' tradition as a major coaster park. Two vehicles are simultaneously launched and appear to be headed for a head-on collision—at 100 mph. The lowest minimum height requirement means that anybody above 42" can be terrified by this experience, which is definitely not for the faint of heart.

EATERTAINMENT The food here is among the best at any theme park, prices are reasonable, and the beer, which is stored, served, and chilled as only a master brewer can, is as good as it gets. In some cases, it's also free!

SHOPPERTOONITIES Some of the park's best values are in the leather and brass shops of the Moroccan Bazaar. Busch Gardens is also a great place to get safari- and tropical-style clothing as well as Anheuser-Busch logo gear.

THE LAY OF THE LAND Basically, the rides and attractions are in the center and the animal areas are around the perimeter.

Busch Gardens

SERENGETI PLAIN

EDGE OF AFRICA

TIMBUKTU

Midway and Arcade

sthaus

NAIROBI

Kenya Kanteen

Petting Zoo

Elephant Wash

Nairobi Train Station

MYOMBE RESERVE

The Great Ape Domain

CROWN COLONY

Colony Club

Skyride and Monorail Station

Egypt Train Station

EGYPT

N

MOROCCO

Stroller/ Wheelchair Rental

ATM

Lockers

Guest Relations

Marrakesh Theater

Main Entrance

KEY	
	Restaurants
	Rest rooms
—•—	Rail Line
••••	Skyride
– –	Monorail
——	Roller Coaster

Moving clockwise from the main entrance at Morocco, areas include Bird Gardens, Stanleyville, Congo, Timbuktu, Nairobi, and the Crown Colony.

THE FAST TRACK Be prepared to walk a lot. Like the real Africa, Busch Gardens is vast. Dress lightly in clothes you won't mind getting wet. The Congo River Rapids and Stanley Falls leave you soaked; put valuables in resealable plastic bags. More than any other park, Busch Gardens lends itself to my go-left strategy. You enter through Morocco and flow naturally to the right. But if you bear hard left into Morocco, you'll find a small walkway past the Hospitality House through the Bird Gardens. If you enter this way— the way that most people leave—you'll meet minimal crowds early in the day. You'll wind up in Egypt, where crowds will be much sparser than they would have been earlier.

MOROCCO

Don't miss the alligators, the musical performances, and the close-order drills by the Mystic Sheiks Marching Band.

SULTAN'S TENT You'll know you've arrived when you see the scantily clad belly and snake dancers.
Worth-It Rating ★★★★★

MOROCCAN PALACE THEATER Back home, you could pay the full-ticket price to see a world-class ice show like "Hollywood on Ice," presented here. It's a spectacularly costumed

and choreographed tribute to the movies—climaxed, of course, by a Busby Berkeley number.
Worth-It Rating ★★★★

BITES The **Zagora Café** and the adjacent **Boujad Bakery** serve huge pastries and wonderful coffees. Next door, an ice-cream shop dishes up giant waffle cones.

BUYS In the **Moroccan Bazaar,** leather and brass are hand-crafted before your eyes (and customized, if you like). Prices are great, especially on leather. On more than one occasion, I have traveled to Busch Gardens just to shop for it.

THE BIRD GARDENS

In the mid-60s, when I first started coming here, these beautifully landscaped gardens were the main attraction, along with the brewery tour, which is now just a memory, and the bird show. Thousands of species of colorful tropical flowers and foliage are identified by name for those who care to know, and beautifully displayed for everyone else.

BIRD SHOW THEATER After all these years, the hourly exotic bird show has changed little. Trainers interact with several species of parrots and other tropical birds and explain where each bird comes from and its markings, characteristics, and habits. The birds do a number of charming fetch-its.
Worth-It Rating ★★★★

ANHEUSER-BUSCH HOSPITALITY CENTER Free beer here! Plus pizza, sandwiches, snacks, live entertainment, and an excellent view of the park.

LAND OF THE DRAGONS

One of the best children's play areas anywhere, this land is a world of giant children's tree houses, where kids can climb, explore, and slide.

DRAGON FLUME RIDE A delightful, kid-sized version of the park's trademark flume rides. Small children who are old enough to walk but still under 56 inches can ride a dragon upstream and over the falls.
Worth-It Rating ★★★★★

STANLEYVILLE

Don't miss the beautiful gardens of the Orchid Canyon; there's a spectacular view from the Tanganyika Tidal Wave.

TRANS-VELDT RAILROAD On the narrow-gauge choo-choo that chugs its way around the park, you get the most extensive view of the African Veldt, if not necessarily the best. The train also gets you around the park.
Worth-It Rating ★★★★★

TANGANYIKA TIDAL WAVE The truth is that I liked Stanley Falls fine until I tried this bigger, better variation. The much larger ride vehicle at this splash-a-rama holds 24 (or more, with small children). Don't be fooled by the long, leisurely cruise—it ends with a 55-foot plunge, the equivalent of a fall from a six-story building. You WILL get soaked.
Worth-It Rating ★★★★★

STANLEY FALLS For many years this was the definitive flume ride, with two to four passengers shooting the falls together in a floating log. Okay, it creaks a little, it's kind of slow, and the big drop is not as thrilling as the one on its newer cousin next door. But it does have character.
Worth-It Rating ★★★★

BITES Some of the park's best food is here. At the **Smokehouse** you'll find barbecued chicken and ribs. At the **Bazaar Café** the specialty is a generous barbecue sandwich.

CONGO

When you travel deep into the Congo, don't miss the view of Claw Island, home of Busch Gardens' majestic white tigers. There's also a Trans-Veldt Railroad station here.

PYTHON Busch Gardens' original steel coaster loops you over twice, but it ends so quickly!
Worth-It Rating ★★★★

SANDSTORM A thrilling high-speed Tilt-A-Whirl-type ride.
Worth-It Rating ★★★

UBANGA-BANGA Regular amusement-park bumper cars, plain and simple.
Worth-It Rating ★★★

CONGO RIVER RAPIDS Accompanied by music that takes you straight to the world of Indiana Jones, Florida's best water ride has you floating down white-water rapids in a 10-passenger raft made from a monster truck tire. You may recall the Greek myth of Tantalus, whose punishment was to spend eternity with an unquenchable thirst, inches from water he could never reach. That's how you'll feel in the interminable line to ride. To keep cool, I soak my T-shirt. I know I'll be soaked when I get off, anyway.
Worth-It Rating ★★★★★

KUMBA Two double-upside-down loops and 13 upside-down turnovers make this coaster truly impressive. It's also one of the longest and most exciting rides in the country.
Worth-It Rating ★★★★★

BITES The **Vivi Storehouse Restaurant,** between the Monstrous Mamba and Ubanga-Banga, sells fast food. An ice-cream stand at the base of the Python serves cold treats.

TIMBUKTU

We call it Timbuk-3 (as in, a little farther than Timbuk-2), because by the time we get this far, we're ready for the park's best eatertainment stop. In addition to the amusements below, there are some good toddler rides.

DOLPHIN THEATER Anheuser-Busch also owns Sea World, so they put on a good dolphin show here. It's amazing how they train these mammals to swim! They also jump, fetch, sing, dance, kiss the trainer, and eat a lot of raw fish.
Worth-It Rating ★★★★

MIDWAY AND ARCADE This may be the only midway you'll ever visit where you feel that someone actually wants you to win something. You pay extra, but you win: We've won at least half a dozen life-size stuffed animals here.
Worth-It Rating ★★★★★

SCORPION If roller coasters are your thing, this single-loop thing is your coaster. You zip through all 360 degrees of the loop, hanging 100% upside down all the way.
Worth-It Rating ★★★★★

BITES In **The Festhaus,** a replica of a German beer hall the size of an aircraft hangar, you lunch next to total strangers at long wooden tables. German dancers, singers, and oompah bands entertain. Portions are generous, prices are reasonable, and the beer is the best.

NAIROBI

On a hot day, you'll envy the Asian elephants as they bathe in Nairobi's cool waterfall. A petting zoo allows kids of the human kind to meet the animals they're named for—friendly, playful young goats—along with other gentle farm animals. There's another Trans-Veldt Railroad station, too.

ANIMAL NURSERY TOUR There's always a new population of adorable babies here. We have seen eagles and other rare birds, some of the park's endangered wild and African deer, and plain old baby critters just opening their eyes.

Worth-It Rating ★★★★★

CURIOSITY CAVERNS Busch Gardens has turned the clock upside down in this habitat for nocturnal creatures. By leaving the lights on at night, they allow visitors a rare glimpse into the habits of several species of bats and nocturnal reptiles. Dad can play Batman, and you'll learn why bats may be the environmental answer to mosquito control.

Worth-It Rating ★★★★ Add 1 if bats don't give you the creeps.

MYOMBE RESERVE Just call this "Gorillas in Our Midst," although the mist is here, too—a cool fog covers the place. At this one-of-a-kind colony of African gorillas, glass walls offer the kind of views of these animals previously available only to Jane Goodall. With its educational audio-video narrative, this is definitely worth a visit.

Worth-It Rating ★★★★★

BITES The **Kenya Kanteen** is the area's fast-food stop, right next to the elephants and the petting zoo.

THE AFRICAN VELDT AND THE SERENGETI PLAIN

Busch Gardens' zoological park contains literally thousands of species with over 40 on the National Wildlife Federation's endangered list. Lions and tigers and bears, oh my! You'll find camels, giraffes, water buffalo, elephants, antelope, and much more—it's a jungle out there! Three rides offer different views of this magnificent attraction.

MONORAIL By far the best way to see the animals is on this aerial adventure. The narration gives you details about the habitats and habits of every species along with occasional anecdotes about landmark births in captivity. We've brought both Tiffany and Ricky frequently since infancy, and I believe this park has sparked an intense interest in animals that will remain with them for the rest of their lives. Unlike the other rides that traverse the park, the monorail lets you off right back where you started.
Worth-It Rating ★★★★★

SKYRIDE This cable car ride takes you over the Serengeti to Stanleyville, the park's thrill center. It also offers an aerial view of the whole layout and makes for spectacular videos.
Worth-It Rating ★★★★ Subtract 1 if the line is too long, as it often is.

CROWN COLONY

We've already covered the monorail and skyride, each of which you can access here. But there's more.

CLYDESDALE HAMLET Anheuser-Busch's Clydesdales are stabled here. Trainers are on hand to tell you about them.

Worth-It Rating ★★★★ Add 2 if you have a horse lover like our Tiffany in tow.

BITES The second-story **Crown Colony House,** with its great picture windows, gives you an excellent view of the Veldt; it's the park's fancy restaurant and has a wine list that's impressive for a theme park. The best deal we've found is on the excellent fried chicken. Seating is first come, first served.

EGYPT

AKBAR'S ADVENTURE TOURS Simulator rides are obligatory at theme parks. This newcomer, a tour of Egypt, is not only exciting, with the usual quota of bumps and crashes, but also funny. Martin Short is hilarious as the used-car salesman of the desert. It's a bit unnecessarily rough for my taste.
Worth-It Rating ★★★★

SAND DIG Establishing Busch Gardens as among the most kid-friendly of theme parks, this sandbox with an ancient theme lets tykes dig, and dig, and dig.
Worth-It Rating ★★★

KING TUT'S TOMB There's no curse on this reproduction of Tut's three-room tomb—spectacularly detailed right down to the burial chamber containing Tut's sarcophagus—as it looked to Professor Carter's ill-fated expedition in 1923. It's a must-see, if only because everyone should visit their mummy.
Worth-It Rating ★★★★★

MONTU You start with your legs dangling over a pit of live crocodiles! If that's not scary enough, cars on this inverted coaster hang from the track rather than sit on top of it, and reach speeds over 60 mph with a G-force of 3.85, as you're flipped topsy-turvy. It's the world's largest coaster of its kind.
Worth-It Rating ★★★★★

chapter 6

THE MAGIC KINGDOM

Walt Disney World

Take I–4 to Exit 25B, labeled for the Magic Kingdom/U.S. 192.

Add 1 if you have children under 10. Subtract 1 if you've been there before and going again makes you skip another park you've never seen.

When they think of Central Florida theme parks, most people think first of the Magic Kingdom. It was the first of the Florida Disney parks and is still loved by millions. Since it opened in 1971, nearly five years after the death of Walt Disney—whose dream it was and who acquired all the land—it has changed little. It was patterned after California's Disneyland, the first true American theme park. Although the Magic Kingdom is similar to Disneyland, there are many differences. Disneyland occupies 80 acres, the Magic Kingdom over 100. Disneyland is surrounded by commercial enterprises owned by others; of the 45 square miles that surround the Magic Kingdom, much is wilderness and all is owned by the Disney company.

While most of Disneyland's rides and attractions are also at WDW, they are not all in the Magic Kingdom. Star Tours, first built at Disneyland, is in the Disney–MGM Studios theme park at Walt Disney World.

The Magic Kingdom's biggest drawback is its age. The concepts for many of its attractions were originally devised by Walt Disney over 50 years ago. Audio-Animatronics, the computer-controlled system of hydraulics responsible for animating many of the robots, were dazzling in the mid-1950s, when they debuted. But they're almost nostalgia pieces now. For little kids, the Magic Kingdom is still the number one WOW!-inspiring place on this earth. For those of us with a little more life experience, it may seem dated.

WHAT'S NEW? Kids can now meet their favorite characters at scheduled times in the area formerly occupied by 20,000 Leagues Under the Sea. Take Flight and Mr. Toad's Wild Ride have been replaced by Buzz Lightyear's Space Ranger Spin and The Many Adventures of Winnie the Pooh, respectively. The Tropical Serenade is now The Enchanted Tiki Room. The Tiki Birds remain, but the show has been updated with hip new music and a hilarious story featuring the voice of Gilbert Gottfried.

TIMING I usually average an attraction every 45 minutes. But even if you hit two adventures an hour, it takes more than two days to see this park—when it's open extended hours.

EATERTAINMENT Our family tries to eat outside the gates, where meals cost half as much. But sometimes we have no choice. A couple of restaurants in the Magic Kingdom require reservations, including a character meal in Cinderella Castle; to book, call 407/WDW–DINE.

The Magic Kingdom

KEY
🍴 Restaurants
🚻 Rest rooms
— Rail Line
••••• Skyride
═══ Monorail

SHOPPERTOONITIES If your schedule is really jam-packed, you may not have time to shop elsewhere. And some things are simply not available outside the gates. The highlight of many vacations is the photo of the family (in mouse ears) in front of Cinderella Castle.

PARADES AND FIREWORKS In addition to attractions, the Magic Kingdom has lots of street entertainment and a few sit-down shows. There are also several parades, which start in Town Square, head down Main Street, then meander through Frontierland; our favorite viewing spot is from the Mile Long Bar in Frontierland—you're right next to the parade route and you can sit, munch, and sip and still see it all. For parade and show times, check the brochure you get when buying your ticket, pick up a schedule at City Hall, or call 407/824–4321 in advance.

The Daily Parade: Even the least of these is as exciting as any parade anywhere. The floats are dazzling, the characters are the ones you know and love, and the music jams. Whatever the theme, start time is 3 PM, weather permitting.★★★★

Mickey's Very Merry Christmas Parade: Between Thanksgiving and New Year's, you'll see Mickey as Santa instead of the daily parade.★★★★★

Main Street Electrical Parade: In this fabulous nighttime parade, millions of lights adorn Disney characters and floats as they move down Main Street. Outside peak seasons, see it as early as 6:15; in peak seasons, at 8 and 10 or 9 and 11. ★★★★★

Fantasy in the Sky Fireworks: A rousing soundtrack accompanies fireworks above Cinderella Castle—one of the world's largest and most dazzling displays. In the early days, it was an occasional thing. Over the years, the show has become increasingly important to the daily schedule. You can see it from virtually anywhere in the park. My most memorable viewpoints are all up high: the top of the Astro Orbiter, the Monorail, and the Skyway. Being in the right place at the right time is purely a matter of luck. Start time is as early as 7 (later during busy periods).★★★★

THE LAY OF THE LAND In the Magic Kingdom, there are seven lands with more than 50 attractions. Main Street USA leads from the entrance turnstiles and Town Square to the so-called Hub, in the shadow of Cinderella Castle. Ranged around the Hub are Adventureland, Frontierland, Fantasyland, Mickey's Toontown Fair, Tomorrowland, and Liberty Square. Each has attractions, shows, eateries, and shops.

THE FAST TRACK In other parks, I advise you to travel clockwise. This is for the simple reason that most people are right-handed and bear right wherever they go. My theory is to go the way other people don't. Because of the design of the Magic Kingdom, with Cinderella Castle in the middle, many people head straight into Fantasyland. Others head left into Adventureland. The least conspicuous route is the walkway into Tomorrowland, and this is where I suggest you begin. Since you always want to start with a busy ride so that you miss the longest lines, head first for Space Mountain or Alien Encounter. Then tour counterclockwise, ending in Adventureland, seeing attractions in the order below.

Another strategy of ours is to take the Walt Disney World Railroad straight to Mickey's Toontown Fair. Then we head into Fantasyland, followed by Liberty Square, Frontierland, Adventureland, and, finally, Tomorrowland.

Choose what you want to see carefully. Wait times are posted near attractions' queue areas, and message boards parkwide list entertainment and character appearance times.

MAIN STREET USA

This old-fashioned street full of shops is busiest right before and after parades and at the end of the day.

WALT DISNEY WORLD RAILROAD Real antiques dating from the turn of the century, these little engines pull you around the perimeter of the Kingdom, with stops at Main Street, Frontierland, and Mickey's Toontown Fair. In a way, this train planted the seed that started the whole theme-park concept: It was Walt's desire to expand the ride-on scale-model train he had built at home for himself and his daughters that inspired him to create Disneyland. Here, when there's not much of a line, the train is a quick way into the heart of the Magic Kingdom. It is also a great place to videotape most of the park in one easy step. You can shoot a quick flick, stop at Mickey's Toontown Fair (the only place where you're guaranteed a photo op with the reigning rodent), shoot the kids with Mickey, then come back to the station and drop your camera in a locker.

Worth-It Rating ★★★★

MAIN STREET CINEMA *Steamboat Willie,* the first Mickey Mouse cartoon and Disney's first talkie, is featured here in an old-time movie theater. Dom Deluise leads a star-studded cast in *Mickey's Big Break,* a film about how Mickey got the part. There's no waiting and it's cool on a hot day.

Worth-It Rating ★★★ Add 1 if you're a nostalgia buff.

MAIN STREET VEHICLES Several old-time vehicles, including a vintage fire engine and trolleys pulled by gigantic horses, take you one-way down Main Street.

Worth-It Rating ★★★ Add 2 if there's no wait.

BITES **Tony's Town Square Restaurant** recreates the site of one of the most romantic moments in motion-picture history, the passionate spaghetti kiss in *Lady and the Tramp.* Naturally, the cuisine is Italian. The decor is Italian-caricature, all stained glass and ceiling fans. Reservations are essential. At snack time, hit the **Main Street Bake Shop,** for Toll House cookies, or the **Plaza Ice Cream Parlor** for two scoops. I wish I could count the times I've stopped at **Casey's Corner** for a hot dog and Casey at the keyboard. It's on the corner as you turn off Main Street toward Adventureland. At the **Plaza Restaurant,** at the Hub end of Main Street, the theme is turn-of-the-century and the food is deli-style. Reservations are recommended. The **Crystal Palace,** probably the best dining deal in the park, serves an all-you-can-eat lunch and dinner buffet with carved meats, hot vegetables, and a salad bar; characters are on hand then and at breakfast. One of the most common questions I've been asked about the Magic Kingdom is "What's in Cinderella Castle?" The answer is **Cinderella's Royal Table.** You'll find steak and seafood at lunch and dinner and Disney characters (plus early admission to the park) for breakfast. Reserve ahead (tel. 407/WDW–DINE).

ENTERTAINMENT The **Dapper Dans**, Main Street's rib-tickling barbershop quartet—complete with straw hats—sing your favorites in tight harmonies. The brass-and-drum **Walt Disney World Marching Band** plays old-time and contemporary music. The **Rhythm Rascals** are an old-fashioned ragtime band. Finally, on the Magic Kingdom's main stage, below Cinderella Castle, you'll often find the **Kids of the Kingdom** singing and dancing up a storm.

BUYS Shopping is really the biggest attraction on Main Street. Little stores line both sides of the road. Many people don't realize that though they all look like individual storefronts on the outside, the stores are actually open to one another inside. So on hot days, you can walk almost from one end of the street to the other in air-conditioned comfort by cutting through the stores.

The **Firehouse Gift Station** sells character toys and clothing with a firehouse theme. **Disneyana Collectibles** is where you can sign your name in the Magic Kingdom guest book. If you see the name "Michael Eisner" on the page, that's probably me. The shop sells real and reproduced animation cels, figurines, and other Disney art and collectibles. The **Emporium** is the largest and most complete of the stores in the Magic Kingdom. Dominating Main Street at the Town Square end, it sells just about everything Disney. Where can you get your own monogrammed set of Mickey Mouse ears? The **Chapeau** is it! Only $5 plus tax, the hats used to be available only in basic black. Now, they come in a variety of colors and styles. Mine says "Annette" (really!). The **Main Street Camera Center**, the park's central camera store, stocks film, tapes, and accessories. They also sell and rent cameras, including video cams. You'll be surprised how much you can spend in **Disney Clothiers**—or maybe not. The **Main Street Confectionery** and **Market House** sell lots of sweets. **Uptown Jewelers,** the Tiffany & Company of the theme park, stocks Disney jewelry. How about a gold Mickey Mouse watch? I actually own one. You could easily blow the kids' college money on jewel-encrusted characters and other goodies. The **Main Street Athletic Shop** will sell you that Minnie Mouse workout suit you've been wanting. **Disney & Company** is a children's clothing and toy store. In the **Shadow Box**, silhouette artists snip portraits of your loved ones. You can watch glassblowers at work in **Crystal Arts.** Just keep a close rein on your littl'uns.

One of the bonuses of coming to WDW over Christmas is on Main Street, where every year shop windows display spectacularly animated tableaux depicting Disney features. It takes me back to when I was a little kid and one of the highlights of the season was a visit to the wonderful animated windows at Macy's in New York. I bring my kids here every year to re-create that experience for them.

TOMORROWLAND

For the last few years I have felt that Tomorrowland was what we used to think the year 2000 would be like back in the 1950s. Now, the redesigned Tomorrowland is the freshest and brightest spot in the Kingdom—and a great place to start.

THE TIMEKEEPER Robin Williams plays the robot emcee of this film, which combines Disney's CircleVision 360 filming technique with Audio-Animatronics technology to create an adventure in which a typical family interacts with legendary sci-fi writers and time-travel experts Jules Verne and H. G. Wells. Well done! The special effects are brilliant!

Worth-It Rating ★★★★★

EXTRATERRORESTRIAL ALIEN ENCOUNTER The story is that an interplanetary spacecraft is foolishly transporting some dangerous alien life forms. Guess what? They get loose and slime you! Universal's Terminator 2: 3D is a better execution of a similar concept. Still, this update of the hopelessly dated Mission to Mars attraction is a real romp!

The Fast Track: Try to hit this attraction when the waiting room is about half full. All seats are good. Timid children *will* be frightened—but mine love it.

Worth-It Rating ★★★★★

BUZZ LIGHTYEAR'S SPACE RANGER SPIN In this ride, based on the spaceman from *Toy Story,* your car turns 360 degrees as you fire your laser at moving targets. It's a howl!

The Fast Track: Lines generally move quickly. This is an easy one to get on and off, and well worth the time.

Worth-It Rating ★★★★★

ASTRO-ORBITER This is the old Star Jets, like Dumbo without the ears, except here you're extra high because the boarding area is one flight up, accessible via elevator. The high point is that it's a WDW high point—with a great view!

Worth-It Rating ★★ Add 1 if the lines are short. Add 3 if you can time your ride to catch the fireworks.

TOMORROWLAND TRANSIT AUTHORITY Once known as the PeopleMover, this little train takes you on an electromagnetic track around Tomorrowland and through Space Mountain. Very relaxing.

Worth-It Rating ★★ Add 1 if you're tired.

CAROUSEL OF PROGRESS This was originally at the 1964 New York World's Fair and has been in continuous operation since then. More people have been on it than any other ride or show anywhere, ever. The technology and concept are a little dated, but the show still holds up. You board a moving theater in the round. As the seats move past each scene, you measure the scientific progress of humanity in this century by the changes in household appliances.

Worth-It Rating ★★★

SKYWAY TO FANTASYLAND I never could figure out why this ride was designed to take such a long route to go a short distance. Still, it's your best chance to get aerial video or still photos of the parks.

The Fast Track: The line is usually shorter in Tomorrowland.

Worth-It Rating ★★★ Add 1 if the line is short.

SPACE MOUNTAIN The world's premier roller coaster is entirely in the dark, with shooting stars overhead. It's also one of the best and most enduringly popular rides at WDW.

The Fast Track: The lines are long. Check the line to the left; sometimes it's shorter. Kids must be 44 inches tall to ride. Don't bother if you get sick easily, are pregnant, or have a weak heart or bad back.

Worth-It Rating ★★★★★

TOMORROWLAND SPEEDWAY Cars on tracks, no race, no passing, no point. The lines are long, and it's all hot and smelly—I always say that the EPA should close it down because of the air quality. Besides, it's really dated. Go only if the kids won't let you get away. A better bet with the same idea is the Sega race course at Epcot's Innoventions. The simulators there *feel* real, and the race *is* real.

The Fast Track: Kids must be at least 44 inches tall to drive.

Worth-It Rating ★★

BITES On the days that we arrive in the Magic Kingdom hungry, the place that usually stops us is the **Plaza Pavilion**, a fast foodery that serves pizza and chicken strips. The big windows offer an excellent view of Tomorrowland. Live shows at nearby Rocket-Tower Plaza make it even more enjoyable. **Auntie Gravity's Galactic Goodies**, near the Tomorrowland Speedway, is a pit stop for frozen yogurt and fruit juices. At **Cosmic Ray's Starlight Cafe**, burgers and chicken headline one of the best fast-food menus in the Kingdom. The **Lunching Pad** at Rocket-Tower Plaza, a little hot-dog stand, is at the base of the Astro Orbiter, right across from Space Mountain.

BUYS **Merchant of Venus** wins my award for the most creatively named store in the park. Just outside Alien Encounter, it specializes in extraterrestrial souvenirs—trinkets with holograms, toy rockets, and other space thingies. **Geiger's Counter,** which has another one of those great names, is one of a couple of places in the Kingdom where you can get your monogrammed mouse-ears hat.

MICKEY'S TOONTOWN FAIR

This is the only place in the park where you can count on meeting up with the world's most famous Mouse. Bring your camera and your autograph book and stand in line for a minute with the Mickster. Be ready—cast members try to keep the line moving—and don't ask any tough questions. Mickey, like all Disney characters, is mute. He's allowed to nod, shake his head, and shrug his shoulders.

Replacing Mickey's Starland, which opened as Mickey's Birthdayland for Mickey's 60th birthday in 1988, Toontown was revamped in 1996, and, as a result, now reflects Disney Imagineers' four decades of experience in creating theme-park fun. Toontown is easy to get around in and gives you a lot to do with minimum waiting.

Worth-It Rating ★★★ Add 2 if you're traveling with children under 10.

MICKEY'S COUNTRY HOUSE Mickey's cartoon world comes alive here. The furniture and Mickey's personal effects are all larger than life. You'll see the Great One's bedroom, his sports equipment, his photos, and his Goofy-remodeled kitchen. When you leave, you're headed straight for the Toontown County Fair, where you have an appointment with the Toontown Fair's chief magistrate, Judge Mickey!

MINNIE'S COUNTRY HOUSE The collection of arts and crafts, the charmingly rustic interior, and the manicured garden portray Minnie as Martha Stewart with big ears. Out back, she greets visitors in her garden gazebo.

DONALD'S BOAT In this wet little playground in the middle of the attractions area, kids can climb and slide on Donald's leaky boat. Little jets of water squirt everywhere, giving kids a chance to cool off on hot days. Personally, I'm neither too old nor too stuffy to stand in the jets myself on a hot day and soak myself well enough to stay cool for several hours. You're at Disney World—be a kid!

TOON PARK Foam animals and a padded floor are lower maintenance than the live animals of the petting zoo that used to be here (I miss Minnie Moo, the cow with the mouse-ears shape on her hide). Kids like climbing on the large, padded animals and bouncing on the thick foam carpet.

THE BARNSTORMER AT GOOFY'S WISEACRES FARM The park has needed a ride like this for years—a kid-sized coaster that takes people who can't reach the height bars at the other thrill rides on a barnstorming flight that crashes right through Goofy's giant red barn.

TOONTOWN FAIR TRAIN STATION This is a great place to get on or off the Magic Kingdom's antique train. The station is large and spacious and you seldom have to wait.

BUYS The **Duck County Courthouse** sells souvenirs of *Duck Tales* and "Disney Afternoon." At the giant **Toontown Fair Hall of Fame,** you can send Florida citrus—or collect an autograph and photo with famous characters from classic Disney feature cartoons.

FANTASYLAND

A tribute to the early Disney cartoon classics on which the studio's feature business was based, this land is dominated by Cinderella Castle, where gingerbread architecture and cobblestone streets create a cartoon view of medieval Europe, where fairy tales began.

MAD TEA PARTY This giant replica of the Mad Hatter's tea cups from *Alice in Wonderland* is one of my family's favorites. You spin around so fast that you get dizzy. (Okay, so it's a dressed-up carnival standard. But it's a great old carnival ride, with Disney music and decor that make it special.)
Worth-It Rating ★★★★

THE MANY ADVENTURES OF WINNIE THE POOH We'll miss Mr. Toad, who used to reside here. Now, Pooh, Tiffany's favorite character, receives some long-deserved attention in this mild kiddy ride. You take Pooh's honey pot through the 100-acre wood, encountering Pooh's friends along the way.
Worth-It Rating ★★★★ Add 1 for small kids or true Pooh fans.

SNOW WHITE'S ADVENTURES The wicked Queen used to scare the heck out of my kids—and apparently they weren't the only ones, because she's nearly gone now. Still fairly low-tech, the ride now shows you more of the dwarfs.
Worth-It Rating ★★★ Add 1 if you have kids under 10.

CINDERELLA'S GOLDEN CARROUSEL A great big old-fashioned merry-go-round with hand-carved wooden horses that go round and round and up and down to the tunes of famous Disney classics. I think a carousel is a pretty mundane ride for a place like the Magic Kingdom, but the kids really love this ride, and like everything else at Disney, it's world-class.

Worth-It Rating ★★★★ Add 1 if you like carousels.

DUMBO THE FLYING ELEPHANT This ride with elephant-shaped cabs was part of the inspiration for my Worth-It Ratings. Though Disney video has turned this ride into an icon, it's really just a standard carnival ride—a pretty short one at that, considering that the wait is almost always long.

Worth-It Rating ★★★ Subtract 2 if you don't have kids. Stay away unless your kids REALLY love Dumbo *and* the line is short.

LEGEND OF THE LION KING One of the new generation of Disney theater shows, this is just terrific. Life-size puppet figures, great costumes, and dazzling special effects bring the popular movie and its characters to life.

The Fast Track: See my tip about not lining up in Chapter 1. Or you'll have to wait in lion like everybody else.

Worth-It Rating ★★★★★

PETER PAN'S FLIGHT From the time she first spoke, my daughter Tiffany loved the story of Peter Pan. So we've spent many hours waiting to board a pirate ship for this flight from the Darling children's bedroom over Neverland. Too bad. Disney's excellent cartoon adaptation of Sir James M. Barrie's timeless tale deserves a better representation than this tired relic of 1950s technology. Also, the lines are too long, and the ride far too short. So sorry.

Worth-It Rating ★★ Add 1 if the line is short, 1 more if your kids are true Peter Pan lovers like Tiffany.

IT'S A SMALL WORLD If you're prone to having silly tunes stuck in your head, beware! (Or wear earplugs!) You cruise the Small World's waterways as too-cute wooden children on either side of you sing their song over and over—first in English, then in every language spoken since the Tower of Babel. Subtly educational, it's also probably one of the most efficiently designed and best-run attractions anywhere. The lines move nicely, and you wait in air-conditioned comfort.
The Fast Track: Look to the left on the ramp as you go down to the boats. Yes, that's a line—and there's often no one in it!
Worth-It Rating ★★★★★

SKYWAY TO TOMORROWLAND The Skyway goes both ways (*see* Tomorrowland), but I like this Swiss wood-shingled station better than the concrete edifice at the other end (and so, apparently, do a lot of other people, because the line is usually longer here).
Worth-It Rating ★★★ Add 1 if the line is short.

BITES Wait! Check out the **Enchanted Grove**. Here's yet another place to get a frozen citrus slushy thing or an ice cream. **Hook's Tavern**, a corner booth next to Peter Pan's Flight, dispenses soft drinks. **Lumière's Kitchen**, inspired by Jerry Orbach's memorable singing candle in *Beauty and the Beast*, specializes in quick kid's meals. **Mrs. Potts' Cupboard** dishes out soft-serve ice cream, floats, and sundaes. **The Little Big Top** has cold drinks and shakes. **Pinocchio Village Haus**, overlooking It's a Small World, is convenient. Low-fat turkey dogs are the current house specialty.

BUYS Fantasyland shops are all clustered together around the Fantasyland entrance to Cinderella Castle. **Tinker Bell's Treasures** sells children's clothing, including Minnie Mouse dresses and other character outfits. **Mickey's Christmas Carol** is a Christmas store loaded with Disney-theme ornaments. **Fantasy Faire** has stuff from the latest animated releases. The **King's Gallery** is full of medieval-style items. We once bought Tiffany a flowing princess hat here. Like much of our Disney memorabilia, the hat is long gone, but the cherished photo remains. The **Aristocats** sells Disney and other clothing for grown-up children. Pop into **Seven Dwarfs Mining Co.** for anything related to the feature film that catapulted Walt to fame in 1937. Many of the treasures featuring Doc, Sleepy, Dopey, Happy, Bashful, Sneezy, and Grumpy and their young surrogate mother have been staples in Disney merchandising for decades.

LIBERTY SQUARE

HAUNTED MANSION This is a spooktacular experience from beginning to end. Don't miss the funny tombstones near the entrance, with epitaphs like "Here Lies Fred/A Great Big Rock Fell On His Head!" Inside, you walk, then ride, through a collection of scary scenes that feature every special effect in the Imagineers' book. Lots of people ask, in the room that stretches, whether the ceiling is going up or the floor is going down? The answer is yes! (It's not an elevator, as many believe. The ceiling goes up—just as it seems.)

The Fast Track: Stay to the left, especially in the entrance area. Most people form a line, but actually there's just one big open area and people are expected to fill it up in a mass. Because they don't, you can often go right to the front. Even on crowded days, staffers actually have to ask people to move up. So when you do, ignore the curmudgeons scowling at you as you pass. When you get to the stretching room, walk straight across to the exit door, so that you can be the first out into the next queue. This is the line for the ride. You'll stand on a moving conveyor belt and step into a moving car. Everyone will be trying to go right; so follow my tip and pass on the left. You could win several valuable Disney minutes—redeemable at the next attraction.

Worth-It Rating ★★★★★

MIKE FINK KEELBOATS Only Elvis and the Beatles approached the popularity of Davy Crockett as he was depicted by Walt Disney on the *Disneyland* TV show in the 1960s. The episode with Mike Fink and the keelboat race, which this boat ride recalls, was one of the best shows. The Wild West scenery is basically the same as you see from the riverboats, except that your viewpoint is closer to the water. Don't do both unless you're determined to ride every ride.

Worth-It Rating ★★★ Add 1 if there's no line.

LIBERTY BELLE RIVERBOAT If you've never taken a ride on an old paddle wheeler, this is your chance! It's authentic, enlightening, and fun, especially if you do as I do: Jump on board singing "Old Man River," ignore the weird looks from the other passengers, and enjoy the scenery, which looks almost like Missouri. And they really do shout "Mark Twain!"

At night the river pirates come out, so the boats stop running at dark.

Worth-It Rating ★★★ Add 1 if there's no line.

THE HALL OF PRESIDENTS Abe Lincoln and Bill Clinton both speak during this winner, which sums up American history as it was made by the nation's presidents. The enormous panoramic film is followed by a roll call of chief executives. Disney's Audio-Animatronics presidents are very realistic in every detail. Though they do not answer questions from the audience (believe me, I've asked), the show is an asset to any parent trying to inspire an interest in history.

Worth-It Rating ★★★★ Add 1 if you want to give your children a history lesson.

BITES Sleepy Hollow offers vegetarians a nice fast-food menu of salads and sandwiches. My family's favorite fast-food stop in the park? **Columbia Harbour House.** Though fried fish and chicken baskets are the headliners, we go for the rich, hot clam chowder, served in a whole-grain bread bowl. Yummy! There's hearty fare like pot roast at the Colonial-style **Liberty Tree Tavern.** Dinner is with the characters, lunch is without, and both are by reservation only.

BUYS The **Silversmith** sells gifts and jewelry made of silver or pewter. If you've always wanted a cast-pewter Mickey, go no farther. **Heritage House** offers Americana. My little Ricky, a budding Civil War buff, favors it for its excellent selection of Civil War-inspired souvenirs. **Olde World Antiques** specializes in Victorian jewelry and Annette Funicello's own Cello perfume. (Okay, so you've never heard of it. Anyway, it's here.) And remember *The Legend of Sleepy Hollow*? I do! It was spooky with that headless horseman, and it's the theme for **Ichabod's,** a magic store that also sells novelties and costume masks. Hit the **Yankee Trader** for kitchen items.

FRONTIERLAND

Because many of us grew up with Walt Disney, it's easy to forget that he was born at the end of the frontier era. Back then, Buffalo Bill's Wild West Show still toured America as the nation's most famous traveling show. The Old West was a frequent Disney theme. Its depiction in his Davy Crockett shows was one of his biggest successes.

DIAMOND HORSESHOE REVUE Step right into this saloon and have a root beer! Shows are continuous, dance hall girls sing and dance, and rowdy barkeeps tell jokes. It's a good place to mix food and fun.
Worth-It Rating ★★★★ Add 1 if you've decided it's time to buy food in the park.

COUNTRY BEAR JAMBOREE The most fun of all the Audio-Animatronics shows is this Disney version of the Grand Ol' Opry, with 20 full-size singing bears, a moose, and a bison. As many times as we've seen it (dozens), we still howl when Big Al sings "Blood on the Saddle." Lines are reasonable and the waiting air-conditioned, unless the line is out the door.

The Fast Track: Not everybody who's waiting gets into every show, so grab a spot near the doors in the waiting room.
Worth-It Rating ★★★★ Add 1 if the line is extra short.

TOM SAWYER ISLAND In this re-creation of the world of Tom Sawyer and Huck Finn, a real island in the middle of the Magic Kingdom's lagoon, you can crawl through tunnels, scamper over swaying wooden bridges, and "fahr them guns at Fort Sam Clemens!" (The guns make a lot of noise, but don't really shoot anything, by the way.) There's no light on the island, so regardless of park hours, it closes at dusk.
Worth-It Rating ★★★ Add 1 if your kids are old enough to study Mark Twain.

BIG THUNDER MOUNTAIN RAILROAD The premise here is that a mine train has broken loose from the top of an old mine, and you're on a swooping, plunging, out-of-control ride through the mountains and gorges of Wild West mining country. Steam geysers and water add to the effect.
The Fast Track: Kids must be 40 inches or taller to ride. We beat the lines by staying left. There are several water fountains en route; soak your head or your shirt to keep cool.
Worth-It Rating ★★★★ Add 1 if the line is short.

SPLASH MOUNTAIN This water coaster, a combination log-flume ride and Audio-Animatronics adventure is based on *Song of the South,* Disney's take on Joel Chandler Harris's Uncle Remus stories. During your ride with Brer Rabbit, Brer Bear, and Brer Fox, the biggest thrill is the 50-vertical-foot splashdown at the end. The line winds through a maze in the valley beneath the mountain with a few minor sites and sounds like music in the bushes, but Disney could have done a much better job making the line part of the experience. As it is, the lines are long and the wait awful. Still, the ride is so good that the bad wait almost doesn't matter.

The Fast Track: No children under 44 inches tall.

Worth-It Rating ★★★★★

BITES Pecos Bill Café is one of the larger fast-food stops, with a spectacular view of Big Thunder Mountain. Out on the street, a stand sells giant smoked turkey drumsticks. As for the **Mile Long Bar**, it's our favorite place to watch parades. If you arrive early, you can grab a seat under the roof, where you'll have a little shade. Unless you're really late or it's really crowded, though, you'll get a seat.

BUYS Splashdown Photo is the place where you can pick up the photo taken of your family as you plunged down the big drop at the end of the Splash Mountain ride. Even if you don't buy the picture, the instant replay is fun. The **Briar Patch**, also just outside Splash Mountain, sells gifts based on *Song of the South* as well as Winnie the Pooh merchandise. **Big Al's**, just outside Country Bear Jamboree, sells take-home versions of that show's many popular characters. If you're old enough to remember coonskin caps, you'll be glad to know that they still have 'em at several shops. **Prairie Outpost & Supply** sells Native American crafts and *Pocahontas* items. The **Trading Post** specializes in Western accessories and the **Trail Creek Hat Shop** sells hats from one to a full ten gallons. **Frontier Wood Carving** will put your name in oak.

ADVENTURELAND

THE ENCHANTED TIKI ROOM—UNDER NEW MANAGE-MENT This attraction just received a much needed revamp. In the new show, *Aladdin*'s Iago and *The Lion King*'s Zazu compete for control of the all-new singing bird show. The new show is funny and hip, while still retaining the charm and infectious melody of the original.
Worth-It Rating ★★★★★

PIRATES OF THE CARIBBEAN Also from Disneyland, this is another welcome spot on a hot day. The lines wind through a fake dungeon that's damp, cool, and full of interesting details that stay with the theme. Then you board a pirate boat that takes you on a wild adventure, through an artillery battle and scenes of a drunken carousing (the pirates, not you). *The Fast Track:* Here, even the wait is great. But time after time we skip the entire line just by keeping left.
Worth-It Rating ★★★★★

JUNGLE CRUISE This is one of the original Disneyland rides—I remember watching the film of its construction on Walt's TV show back in the mid-50s. The jungle props, plaster pachyderms, and amazing menagerie of other motorized mammals still hold up well after all these years. An open-sided, gas-powered steamer takes you along the Nile and through Southeast Asia, South Africa, and the Amazon rain forest, not necessarily in that order. Watch out for the squirting elephant. Some of the skippers drone, but when they take their comedy seriously, their monologues can be a hoot!

The Fast Track: The winding queue is well concealed and can be the park's worst wait on a hot, muggy day. Before committing yourself to an hour of sweat, park a family member in line while you check out the waiting time. If it's too long, come back in the evening when it's cooler. If the park isn't open late, ride as early as possible.

Worth-It Rating ★★★★ Subtract 1 if the line is long.

SWISS FAMILY TREEHOUSE Disney's film *Swiss Family Robinson* has enjoyed a revival thanks to exposure on the Disney Channel and on video to a whole new generation of kids. So you may want to check out this replica of the house high in a banyan tree that appeared in the movie. My family is afraid of heights, so the steep open climb isn't our cup of tea. Apart from that, I don't think it's worth the wait. You don't do anything and neither does the tree house—you just look at it.

Worth-It Rating ★★ Add 1 if the line is short and you're not acrophobic.

BITES At **Aloha Isle,** the offerings are fruit-juice-based, and shakelike. This is what the tropics are for! In **El Pirata y el Perico,** there's a pirate theme and Mexican fast food like tacos. **Sunshine Tree Terrace** serves more frozen juice concoctions—these made of indigenous citrus.

BUYS Most shops cluster in an ersatz bazaar. Stop at **Bwana Bob's** if you just can't live without a stuffed tropical bird. Check out **Elephant Tales** for safari-theme gifts and clothing, **Traders of Timbuktu** for things African. The **Tropics Shop** is your source for Hawaiian shirts and other cliché tropical attire. And stop by the **Zanzibar Shell Co.** for sea shells and shell crafts. **House of Treasure,** the **Treasure Chest,** and **Lafitte's** have pirate themes. **Plaza del Sol Caribe Bazaar,** just outside Pirates of the Caribbean, expands your tropical options.

chapter 7

EPCOT

Walt Disney World

Take I–4 to Exit 26B, labeled for Epcot and Rte. 536.

Drop 1 if you have children under 6.

E pcot is a breathtaking, first-class attraction loved by millions. The name is an acronym for "Experimental Prototype Community of Tomorrow," a title said to have been chosen by Walt Disney to herald a planned community similar to Celebration, the new town Disney is finally building in Kissimmee. Insiders know that the initials really stand for "Every Person Comes Out Tired" from this, the biggest of all the theme parks. I love that joke, because for years, this was my least favorite park.

But a funny thing happened while I researched this book. As I went back again and again, the place won me over. Maybe my idea of what a theme park should be was too limited. Perhaps I missed the point by simply looking for rides. Perhaps, being so conscious of value and price, I was overly annoyed by what I perceived as blatant commercialism. Or perhaps my vision was clouded by one too

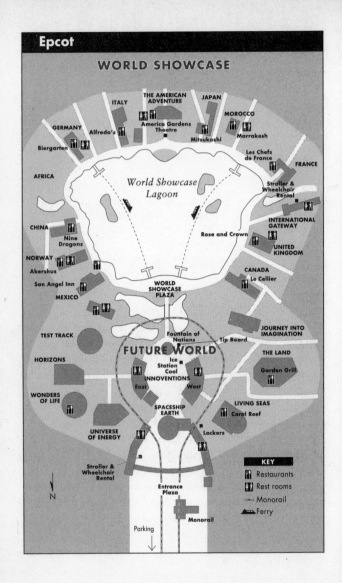

many trips with children who were too young—children who are only now old enough to be excited by the experiences it offers.

Now it's clear to me: Epcot is a place filled with wonder. It may be the only place anywhere that parents can take their children on an instant trip around the world, albeit a fantasy trip, and learn about the cultures of every continent. One can only guess how many future scientists, researchers, and doctors might find, at Epcot, the first spark that ignites their lifelong passion. The bottom line is that Epcot has too many spectacular attractions and wonderful cultural experiences to be ignored.

It is also huge and seldom feels congested, regardless of the day or the season. If you hate theme-park crowds, or if the crowds at the other parks start to get you down, the size may be a plus. And it's ideal on rainy days. Crowds thin out when it rains. And with the right clothes and attitude, you could have the park mostly to yourself.

WHAT'S NEW? After much delay, GM's new Test Track has finally opened, and boy is it a scream. Epcot will be headquarters for WDW's 15-month millennium celebration, beginning in 1999 and running until 2001. Following the park's theme, activities will highlight the history, achievements, and future of humanity.

TIMING One September weekday, when crowds were thin, I went to World Showcase. Mind you, I wasn't even trying to include Future World. Nor did I have kids or family to slow me down. I did not finish before closing time. You won't either. So choose what you want to do carefully. There's far too much at Epcot for a single day.

EATERTAINMENT AND SHOPPERTOONITIES Particularly in World Showcase, food and shopping are an integral part of the experience. So to enjoy many of Epcot's best features, you have to spend more money than in any other park.

THE LAY OF THE LAND Epcot is like a barbell. You enter on the bottom, in Future World, facing Spaceship Earth, Epcot's signature geosphere. Just beyond it, the pavilions of Future World are arranged roughly in a circle around a large, central plaza. Beyond this plaza lies the World Showcase Lagoon, which is ringed by a promenade punctuated by the pavilions of World Showcase. The American Adventure pavilion is directly opposite Spaceship Earth across the lagoon.

THE FAST TRACK Because Future World opens first, I suggest you begin there. Lines will be long if you haven't arrived early. So do the things that don't have lines, such as Innoventions. Head to World Showcase a little before it opens, even if you're not finished in Future World. Start in Mexico and work clockwise to Canada. Remember, the earlier you get to World Showcase, the thinner the crowds will be. (Conversely, crowds thin out at Future World later in the day.)

Future World

SPACESHIP EARTH

SPACESHIP EARTH RIDE Question: Have you wondered what's inside that geosphere, the giant golf ball that is the symbol of Epcot? Answer: A great ride, which squeezes in a brief history of the world from dinosaurs to spaceships.

The Fast Track: You'll often find short lines, particularly late in the day. If you arrive early and it's crowded, skip it and come back before you leave.

Worth-It Rating ★★★★★

INNOVENTIONS EAST AND WEST

What's new in the world? This is where you can see the latest in gimmicks and gadgets and try nifty new things.

Stop in for a multimedia trip through the history of innovation and invention with Bill Nye the Science Guy. Then try out a new wrist telephone from AT&T. Check out the latest software, and play animator on a Silicon Graphics workstation. Have your camcorder handy: At the GE exhibit you can be interviewed by Jay Leno through the magic of electronic special effects. My son, Ricky, could happily spend the entire day at Sega's exhibit. Its full-size road race is a wild, jolting simulator where you can pass, skid, spin out, and actually compete to win against other drivers. Too bad it costs an extra four bucks.

Also check out the live entertainment and the leaping fountains—spurts of water arc through the air in intricate computer-controlled sequences. Everything is high-tech, even the entertainment. Check out **Future Corps** band, the **Kristos Acrobats,** the talking **EpBOTS** robots, and the impromptu, cacophonous, comedic **Jammitors,** who play a mean garbage can. Mickey, Minnie, and other characters show up in metallic, space-age outfits. Signs throughout the park list where they'll be.

Worth-It Rating ★★★★★

BITES Go for sandwiches and chicken at the **Electric Umbrella**, or pasta and pizza at the **Pasta Piazza Ristorante**. **Fountain View** serves espresso and baked goods.

THE LIVING SEAS

The giant aquarium in the middle of the pavilion is not keeping the folks at Sea World up at night, but you'll see a fairly impressive collection of undersea life as well as aquatic exhibits and a ride "through the ocean depths."
Worth-It Rating ★★★

BITES Gazing through the 8-foot glass windows at the popular **Coral Reef Restaurant** is almost like being inside the aquarium. Seafood is on the menu. And if you've ever wanted to see Mickey Mouse underwater, this is the place; he plays diver during the restaurant's character breakfast.

THE LAND

LIVING WITH THE LAND One of those infectious Disney soundtracks follows your craft as you glide along a waterway filled with high-tech gardens that are actually used to grow some of the food you eat in the park. It's fun and informative if you have school-age children.
Worth-It Rating ★★★★

GREENHOUSE TOUR They use hydroponics and other high-tech tricks to grow their own veggies and other things in the greenhouses here; on this 45-minute guided walk, you see how. Whether or not this is worth the trouble depends entirely on your interest in the science of agriculture. Make reservations when you get to the pavilion.

THE HARVEST THEATER In the *Circle of Life*, the harmless film that plays here, the *Lion King* gang talks about taking care of Mother Earth.
Worth-It Rating ★★★

FOOD ROCKS This show is like It's a Small World with singing veggies. Little kids love it.
Worth-It Rating ★★★★

BITES The **Garden Grill**, a revolving full-service restaurant, overlooks some of the scenery you see in the Listen to the Land boat ride. Reserve ahead. The **Sunshine Season Food Fair**, an elaborate food court, gives you home-style cooking with natural and organic ingredients. Try the vegetable lasagna at the **Cheese Store**.

JOURNEY INTO IMAGINATION

This pavilion explores the nature of the creative process.

MAGIC EYE THEATER *Honey, I Shrunk the Audience!*, which plays here, is the best show at Epcot and my pick for second-best 3D show in the world (after Universal's Terminator 2: 3D). A 3D sequel to the films, *Honey, I Shrunk and/or Blew*

Up the Kids and/or the Baby, it gets actor Rick Moranis to shrink the entire audience. You're subsequently menaced by giant reptiles. Don't miss it.
Worth-It Rating ★★★★★

THE IMAGE WORKS A cool playground featuring hands-on experiences with "creative playthings" that demonstrate technology ranging from computer graphics to static electricity.
Worth-It Rating ★★★★

JOURNEY INTO IMAGINATION RIDE Spend a mildly amusing 13 minutes with Figment, the purple dragon who's Epcot's quasi-mascot, and his bearded pal, Dreamfinder.
Worth-It Rating ★★★

TEST TRACK

TEST TRACK RIDE You start with a history of GM testing, going back to Chevrolet in the '20s. Then you tour a modern test facility before your own test drive. It starts out slowly with a a few acceleration, bump, and brake tests. Then you tear out of the pavilion at over 60 mph to finish with a thrilling, high-speed race-car experience.
The Fast Track: Lines are long, but it's worth the wait.
Worth-It Rating ★★★★★

WONDERS OF LIFE

One of our favorite stops at Epcot, this has a large center court full of activities that remind me of Innoventions. But here the themes are life, health, and fitness.

BODY WARS This is a simulator ride, like Star Tours at Disney–MGM Studios, except that you're on an imaginary trip into a human being. Your simulator is shrunk and injected into a person (much as Martin Short is in the movie *Inner Space*). The special effects are thrilling and original, but the family and I agree that this one is a little too rough.
The Fast Track: Children under 48 inches, people with heart and back problems, and women who are pregnant or think they might be are advised not to ride. Avoid it if you don't want to get roughed up. Unfortunately, there's no way to get around the lines except by showing up early or late.
Worth-It Rating ★★★★

CRANIUM COMMAND This absolutely charming and wonderfully funny film and Audio-Animatronics show takes you inside the brain of a 12-year-old boy. The star-studded comic cast includes favorite TV actors as operators of vital organs. One of the best shows at Epcot.
The Fast Track: The entrance is hidden at the back of Wonders of Life, so many people miss the show and lines are often short. Before you get in, you'll be routed into a holding area with a movie. There, look for the doors to the show's theater and get as close to them as you can. All seats are good, but the front is the best.
Worth-It Rating ★★★★★

THE MAKING OF ME After you've seen this movie about how babies develop, you may want to start that little "birds and bees" talk with your kids. Or maybe not. In any case, be prepared. This Martin Short film is fairly explicit, and the fetus footage is graphic.

Worth-It Rating ★★★ Add 2 if you want Martin Short to explain the facts of life to your children.

THE CENTER COURT There are all kinds of great activities here. At the **Coach's Corner,** you can evaluate your golf, tennis, or baseball skills. Your swing is videotaped, then reviewed by pros. **Wondercycles** give a quick little workout (you—not me), along with an instant analysis of the calories burned in various thrilling simulated situations. In the cartoon/live action **Goofy About Health** show, the great Goofy demonstrates why you should get your potato off the couch. The **Anacomical Players** improvise skits about health. The **Lifestyle Revue** gives you the chance to rate the healthiness of your lifestyle (or in my case, the lack thereof). Finally, the **Fitness Fairground** lets you test your six senses (the sixth being your sense of humor). One of the activities is sticking your hand into a hole in a box, then trying to figure out what you're touching. Most people guess wrong.

BITES **Pure and Simple** has health-smart fast food such as waffles, yogurt, sandwiches, and salads.

UNIVERSE OF ENERGY

We love this attraction a little more every time we come! It's even better since it was completely revamped in 1996. Now it features Jamie Lee Curtis and Bill Nye the Science Guy, with a cameo appearance by the late Albert Einstein, in a simulated game of "Jeopardy." The entire auditorium moves on a track through a primeval forest filled with life-size Audio-Animatronics dinosaurs. It's a multimedia extravaganza that's funny, informative, and absolutely spectacular.

Worth-It Rating ★★★★★

World Showcase

This group of pavilions is Disney's ongoing, permanent world's fair, where, in a single day, you can capture Kodak moments in front of most of the world's major landmarks.

Not every country in the world is included. Don't look for politics, either. Even though national governments actually participate in the planning and running of the attractions (perhaps *because* they do), all political content has been removed for your protection.

SHOPPERTOONITIES AND EATERTAINMENT Even if you don't buy anything, take time to browse in the shops. Nowhere else in the world will you find such a diverse sampling of international offerings in a single place. And each pavilion features the country's native cuisine in fast fooderies and great sit-down restaurants. The food is pricey, but the presentations are world-class. Reservations are almost always required (tel. 407/824–4321 for information, tel. 407/939–3463 to reserve).

STREETMOSPHERE Streetmosphere is what Disney calls those roaming costumed characters who help set the mood. Stop now and then to watch them; they're one of the best parts of the park. **World-Class Brass** performs pop music with a little comedy throughout World Showcase. Ditto for the **Junkanoo Bus,** a wildly painted Caribbean contraption that not only plays music but has an on-board bar that serves tropical drinks! (You'll find it in Future World, too.)

THE UNITED KINGDOM

You'll see what's so great about Britain in this miniature replication featuring formal English gardens, a great traditional English herb garden and maze, and a cobblestone street lined with Tudor homes and Victorian buildings. Phone home: The old-fashioned red telephone booths really work (and make a nice photo-op).

BITES At the **Rose & Crown,** you'll find traditional British fare, both in its restaurant section and in the adjacent pub. Here's your big chance to try kidney pie (or stick with fish and chips and the obligatory British brews).

BUYS The **Toy Soldier** sells British toys. **Lords and Ladies** is all perfume and tobacco, the **Tea Caddy** all teas and teapots. **Pringle of Scotland** stocks Scottish woolens. Ever since Ricky saw *Braveheart,* he's been fascinated with Scottish culture. Each clan has its own plaid, and the selection here represents most of them. You'll also find real bagpipes, practice pipes to learn on, how-to tapes, and piper music. The **Magic of Wales** and the **Queen's Table** sell decorative items.

STREETMOSPHERE Check out the **World Showcase Players.** Guests help with the skits. And look for the roving bagpipers. When I told one of them that Ricky wanted to learn to play, we were treated to a 15-minute concert with instruction. **Worth-It Rating ★★★★**

NORWAY

The ornate architecture of a 14th-century Norwegian fortress and a 12th-century stave church make this one of the most visually entertaining spots in World Showcase. The church houses Norwegian art and artifacts.

MAELSTROM My daughter Tiffany's favorite ride in World Showcase is a stormy trip in a Viking ship with great Audio-Animatronics bears and more. But the ending is abrupt; one minute you're in the middle of a stormy northern sea, the next you're climbing out of your boat.

BITES They do a good smorgasbord at **Restaurant Akershus,** with good hot and cold entrées and more herring dishes than you'd ever want. You'll feel like a Viking at the rough wooden tables inside the stone walls of what looks like an ancient Norse castle. Reserve ahead.

BUYS The **Puffin's Roost,** just outside Maelstrom, sells clothing, toys, and candy, including the very popular Freia's Non-Stop, resembling M&Ms. There's also one of the world's most extensive selections of plastic, wood, and ceramic trolls. **Worth-It Rating ★★★★★**

CANADA

Totem poles in a scene straight out of the old Northwest Mountie movies welcome you to the Great White North! Framed by a Disney version of Canadian mountains are a sparkling waterfall and a replica of Ottawa's imposing stone Château Laurier. In the foreground, Disney has re-created British Columbia's spectacularly floral Butchart Gardens.

O CANADA! This movie contains a lot of purple mountains' majesty. I love these CircleVision 360 movies. You're completely surrounded by curved screens, which literally put you in the center of the action. But there are no seats, and nothing but a guard rail to lean on. I'd like the thrilling toboggan ride, the powerful audio, and the spectacular views a whole lot more if I didn't have to stand.

BITES With its big, low stone arches, **Le Cellier** looks like a fancy cellar restaurant, but the hearty prime rib, turkey, and shepherd's pie are served cafeteria style, along with salads and desserts. It's my kind of place—and not a bad deal.

BUYS **Northwest Mercantile** is like a log cabin stocked with Native American crafts. **Le Boutique** sells French-Canadian jewelry, fragrances, and novelties.

STREETMOSPHERE Look for both the **Caledonia Bagpipes** and the **Pipes of Nova Scotia.** You may also run into the **Canadian Comedy Corps,** who remind you how funny Canadians can be.
Worth-It Rating ★★★

FRANCE

Here you enter a charming French neighborhood from the 1600s. The Eiffel Tower, which is also here, may be the park's best photo-op. (It's claimed that the real McCoy is the world's most photographed structure. Who can argue?)

IMPRESSIONS OF FRANCE During this 18-minute wide-screen tour of France, you ride, slide, and fly through Paris and the French countryside to the strains of music by classical French composers, played over an excellent sound system. (See, you *can* sit down at an Epcot movie.)

BITES Wouldn't you expect great French food here? At **Les Chefs de France**, take the spiral staircase to the second floor, where three world-class chefs (Paul Bocuse, Roger Vergé, and Gaston Lenôtre) offer dishes like duck à l'orange and snapper with scallops and crab that are truly awesome. **Bistro de Paris** is our favorite Epcot restaurant. My wife, Terrie, loves the French onion soup, and we both endorse the rack of lamb for two. At **Au Petit Café**, you can just pop in and grab a quiche, a croissant, or a chunk of French bread and cheese. And the pop-up children's menu is adorable. If you arrive late in the evening, the meal comes with a reasonable view of IllumiNations from a comfortable seat. Reserve for all.

BUYS Pâté anyone? Check **Le Mode Français**. For fragrances, it's **La Signature**, for cosmetics the **Guerlain Boutique**, for wine **La Maison du Vin**. **Plume et Palette** has art and crystal (watch the kids—"you break it, you bought it" is the motto). With youngsters, you're better off in **Galerie des Halles** (or maybe not—it sells toys and candy). Look for the *Hunchback of Notre Dame* booth. Where else would it be?

STREETMOSPHERE Gordoon, a clown with a Maurice Chevalier accent, improvises with children and seltzer. It's wet, wild, and wonderful. And although gypsies aren't French, France does have gypsies, as portrayed in *Hunchback*. The **Tzigantzi** troupe performs its songs and dances, while nearby Left Bank portrait artists paint you as you wait.
Worth-It Rating ★★★★

MOROCCO

This is a finely detailed reproduction of the North African cities of Fez and Marrakesh. Fez House and the Nejjarine Fountain are both replicas of famous structures from ancient Morocco, and there's an interesting (if a little sparse) exhibit of Moroccan art. But where's Rick's American Café?

BITES North Africans consider lamb to be the best of all meats. At **Restaurant Marrakesh**, beef, chicken, and fish also go into the couscous, but it's never as good with the substitutions. While you dine, the **Casablanca Fez Belly Dancers and Musicians** gyrate. You'll need reservations.

BUYS Carpets, clothing, and crafts spill out the doors and into the street in true bazaar style. **Marketplace in the Medina, Casablanca Carpets, Tangier Traders,** the **Brass Bazaar, Medina Arts,** and the **Berber Oasis** are great places to pick up handcrafted Moroccan brass and leather goods. At the pavilion's edge, clever Disney marketers have taken advantage of the Mideast connection to set up an *Aladdin* shop.

STREETMOSPHERE Keep your ears open for the folk musicians accompanied by belly dancers. Wow! The **Houzali Troupe** performs in the courtyard by the lagoon—four drums, a flute, and one very nice belly.

Worth-It Rating ★★★ Add 1 if you plan to shop here.

JAPAN

The centerpiece of Epcot's Japan is a spectacular re-creation of a classic Japanese garden. You'll also see a replica of a five-story, 8th-century pagoda, Nara's Temple of Horyuji. An art exhibit is housed in a looming reproduction of an antique stone castle surrounded by a moat. Don't miss the life-size statues of mounted samurai on your way out.

BITES In the **Teppanyaki Rooms,** you sit at tables that wrap around big grills where chefs chop up meat and veggies before your eyes, faster than a samurai. If you've been to Benihana, you know the drill. **Tempura Kiku** specializes in batter-fried fare. Reserve for both of these. **Yakitori House** serves Nipponese fast food. The teriyaki beef and chicken dishes, the yummy red bean dessert, and the children's menu rate a mention. And it's surprisingly inexpensive.

BUYS One of Japan's leading merchants, **Mitsukoshi**, offers the best of the wares from its department stores—great kimonos and Japanese dolls as well as lacquerware, fabrics, karate outfits, samurai swords, jewelry, carvings, paintings, and about a zillion little knickknacks.

STREETMOSPHERE One World Taiko consists of two drummers beating out traditional Japanese tunes. **Matsurizi,** a larger group, also performs Japanese percussive music. The bizarre troupe known as **Cirikili** is made up of "stilt birds"—Japanese actor/acrobats on high stilts who wear mechanical bird contraptions that make them look like warriors astride giant metallic ostriches. Think *Shogun* meets *Star Wars*.
Worth-It Rating ★★★ Add 1 if you plan to eat here.

THE AMERICAN ADVENTURE

The focal point of this pavilion is a magnificent Colonial-style structure that's a little like Philadelphia's Independence Hall and Williamsburg's Governor's Mansion in one, with touches of the White House and the Capitol. The beautiful rose garden outside, inspired by the one at the White House, features varieties named for U.S. Presidents and historical figures. Shaded by stately magnolias and sycamores, the grounds look and feel like colonial Virginia—particularly impressive in tropical Florida.

THE AMERICAN ADVENTURE SHOW This really is the best show in the World Showcase. Audio-Animatronics Ben Franklin and Mark Twain host this dazzling musical half hour. It's Disney's best Audio-Animatronics show, period. The figures are so lifelike that at times they look and sound like real actors. The montage of familiar and poignant scenes from America's past may moisten your eyes, as they do mine.

BITES No funny stuff at the **Liberty Inn.** Strictly American burgers, hot dogs, and fries.

BUYS Hit **Heritage Manor** for cutesy American country-style gifts. The selection of American flag novelties (I collect 'em) is one of the best I've seen anywhere, even rivaling those in Philadelphia and Washington, D.C.

STREETMOSPHERE The **Voices of Liberty** sing a capella in the show waiting area. Or try to catch the **Sons of Liberty**, a traditional fife and drum corps. Check the schedule near the stage at the **American Gardens Theater**, across the promenade from the pavilion, for a list of concerts and celebrity appearances.

Worth-It Rating ★★★★★

MEXICO

A carving of the serpent-god Quetzalcoatl presides over the steps of this imposing reproduction Mayan temple. Inside, there's an impressive display of pre-Columbian art. And in the plaza in the pavilion's center is a large, open shopping area crammed with Mexican novelties. In perpetual twilight, the plaza is always cool and dark—excellent on hot, muggy afternoons. The front steps are one of the better spots from which to watch IllumiNations.

EL RIO DEL TIEMPO The pavilion's main feature is this ride (the name translates as "river of time"), which takes you through representations of the history of Mexico from ancient cultures to the present. It's cool and pleasant, but nothing more, so move on if the wait looks long.

BITES The **San Angel Inn Restaurant,** overlooking the River of Time ride, is one of the park's most romantic spots. Lavish margaritas enhance the mood. On the menu, along with predictable Mexican-American enchiladas and tacos, are unexpected selections like mahi-mahi and grilled shrimp. I call the **Cantina de San Angel** "Taco Tinker Bell" (get it?). Its waterfront veranda is a good viewpoint for IllumiNations, and the kids like the churros—crispy, cinnamon-coated Mexican sweets. I highly recommend the generously sized margaritas. Ricky says that the watermelon juice is the best he's ever had.

BUYS Deep in the interior of the pavilion is the **Plaza de los Amigos,** a faux Mexican street market where you can buy castanets, handmade Mexican dolls, pottery, jewelry, ponchos, straw hats, leather goods, even tequila. At **Artesanias Mexicanas,** Mexican glass blowers make tiny animals and characters in glass as well as big, ornate, overpriced, overblown doojamahickees that are definitely not for kids. You can also buy pottery, candles, and other less destructible crafts.

STREETMOSPHERE **Mariachi Cobre,** a 10-piece horn and string ensemble, serenades guests on the veranda and in the pavilion with the kind of music most of us best remember from old gunslinger and bandito movies. **Huitzilin,** a Native American drum and wind group, involves guests in stories, dances, and songs.
Worth-It Rating ★★★★

ITALY

An ornate fountain and a tall brick tower dominate the classic piazza, a reproduction of St. Mark's Square. Faithful recreations of Venetian bridges lead to gondolas that are permanently moored on the lagoon.

BITES If you've never had fettucine Alfredo perfectly prepared, you should try it at the elegant **L'Originale Alfredo di Roma Ristorante,** a branch of the restaurant that invented it. Strolling musicians serenade you under the spectacular chandeliers, and the fresh pasta is made right before your very mouth. Not a pizza in sight! Reservations a must.

BUYS **Il Bel Cristallo** sells Venetian glass, jewelry, leather, and Capodimonte ceramics—those large, shiny ceramic objects covered with pink flowers and angels made famous by the Home Shopping Network. **La Cucina** stocks Italian edibles, wines, and cooking implements. **Delizie Italiane** sells Italian sweets. Pinocchio anyone? His shop is here, too.

STREETMOSPHERE In the piazza look for **I Cantanapoli,** a street quartet playing all your Neapolitan favorites.
Worth-It Rating ★★★★

GERMANY

A statue of St. George slays a statue of a dragon in the main square, surrounded by the gingerbread rooftops. Walking through, you would swear you had entered a German postcard.

BITES The raucous **Biergarten** has an all-you-can-eat buffet—look for me! The wurst is the best! Roast chicken, dumplings, kraut, and potato salad round out the spread. Imported beers in quart steins that look like pitchers are served to revelers at long, wooden tables. And there's nonstop live oompah music, plus yodeling, a glockenspiel, giant alpine horns, and a serenading saw. **Sommerfest** serves German fast food. Try a brat with kraut, meine frau!

BUYS German shops ring the courtyard. Look for German sweets, beer steins, cuckoo clocks, hand-carved wooden nutcrackers, and other Christmas items. A nutcracker nut from an early age, Ricky certifies the selection as the best he's seen (I certify that it's not the cheapest). Check out **Der Bücherwurm** and its beautiful hand-painted eggs; the stuffed stuff and dolls at **Der Teddybär;** and the fine German crystal at **Kunstarbeit in Kristall.**

STREETMOSPHERE The **Alpine Trio**—guitarist, tuba player, accordionist—appear frequently in the square.
Worth-It Rating ★★★ Add 1 if you want to eat a lot.

CHINA

A garden-ringed Temple of Heaven dominates this pavilion. There's a fine display of ancient imperial art, largely from the collection of Beijing's Palace Museum and San Francisco's Avery Brundage Collection.

THE WONDERS OF CHINA This CircleVision 360 movie skips the sweat shops. But it's Chinese torture to endure this 20-

minute show with no seating—everyone stands. I understand the concept—it's easier to spin around while standing. I just don't like it. But if you don't mind, you may enjoy this lavish production with its wide view of the varied cultures and breathtaking geography of this enormous country.

BITES The beautifully appointed **Nine Dragons** serves regional dishes from all over China. **Lotus Blossom Café** is the place to pick up a quick egg roll, stir-fried beef, or wonton soup. Prices are reasonable, and the food is very good.

BUYS **Yong Feng Shangdian** is China's own Macy's. Much of what you see is predictable—lots of silk and knickknacks. Other offerings are surprising, including the Chinese furniture and several pieces only Michael Eisner could afford.

STREETMOSPHERE In the courtyard, both the **Pu Yang Acrobats** and the **Flying Dragon Variety Troupe** perform feats of balance and agility. **China Si Zhu** is the warmup for *Wonders of China*: A performer tells stories of Chinese history while playing the flute, zither, or dulcimer.
Worth-It Rating ★★★★

ILLUMINATIONS

Mark Fisher, who has created Tina Turner, Rolling Stones, and Pink Floyd shows, has made this nighttime extravaganza faster and hipper, with more lights, music, and fireworks than ever before. The pyrotechnics are amazing. It definitely wows the crowds. Unfortunately, the presentation can't overcome the venue's limitations. No matter where I am, I always feel I'm missing the spectcular parts. When you can see it, what you see is fireworks up high and down low on barges on the water and laser lights dancing on Spaceship Earth and turning it into a giant globe, playing on other Epcot buildings, and lighting up the lagoon, all to the accompaniment of a rousing sound track. I can't even imagine how great it would be if I *could* see everything.

chapter 8

DISNEY–MGM STUDIOS THEME PARK

Walt Disney World

Take I–4 to Exit 26B, marked for Route 536 and Epcot.

★★★★★–

It's very nice, but not quite Universal.

Disney has done an excellent job of reinventing the movie park, a genre created by Universal Studios. Although both movie parks try to capture the spirit of the studios of Hollywood's Golden Age, the 1930s and 1940s, Disney–MGM is not so much a replica of an old-time Hollywood studio as a caricature of one—specifically, the one Disney portrayed so successfully in the film *Who Framed Roger Rabbit*.

The park is wonderfully detailed. As you enter, you'll pass a filling station surrounded by vintage cars, oil cans, gas pumps, and spare parts dating from the 1940s. Across the plaza is an old-looking Hollywood-style bungalow, complete with front porch, presided over by a costumed character known affectionately as Sid Cahuenga. A rotating Mickey stands astride an art-deco globe designating Disney–MGM's Crossroads of the World; beneath the mar-

Disney-MGM Studios Theme Park

KEY
- Restaurants
- Rest rooms

Catastrophe Canyon

Residential Street

NEW YORK STREET

Sci-Fi Dine-In Theater

50's Prime Time Café

ECHO LAKE

Mickey Avenue

ANIMATION COURTYARD

Walt Disney Theater

Hollywood & Vine Cafeteria

Studios Tip Board

Brown Derby

Guest Relations

HOLLYWOOD BLVD.

Hollywood Junction Restaurant Reservations

Entrance Plaza

Lockers

SUNSET BLVD.

Main Entrance

ATM

Fantasmic!

velous mouse's marker, reproductions of Hollywood facades line the street.

What does Disney have to do with MGM? Almost nothing: There's never been a Disney–MGM film. But at the time that corporate raider Kirk Kerkorian was disassembling the old MGM in the 1980s, scattering its parts to the winds, Disney was in need of some extra concept material for its movie park, and the rest is history.

Comparisons are inevitable when you write about two movie parks in the same book. Many of the rides and shows at Disney–MGM are similar to those at Universal Studios Escape, but toned down, with the result that Disney–MGM comes across as Universal Lite. Catastrophe Canyon on the Disney–MGM Studios Backlot Tour and Universal's Earthquake: The Big One are almost identical. But the explosion and flood at Catastrophe Canyon, which take place outdoors at a safe distance, are not nearly as terrifying as those at Universal, which take place indoors. Disney–MGM's Star Tours and Universal's Back to the Future are both simulator rides. But the Back to the Future screen, 90 feet tall, is bigger than a drive-in theater's; the Star Tours screen seems smaller than the one at your local mall's multiplex.

The strengths of the Disney park are its cartoon and children's attractions. Those themed around the late Jim Henson's incredibly popular Muppets and the movie *Honey, I Shrunk the Kids* make the park a must-see for families. Disney's animated films—*Aladdin, Pocahontas, The Lion King, Toy Story, Hunchback of Notre Dame, Hercules,* and now, *Mulan*—have been brought to life with wonderful shows, seen in Orlando only at this park. These shows are among the best in any theme park, with production values that are Broadway-class or better. Another highlight is the streetmosphere: strolling character actors pretending to be silent film stars, agents, and other vintage Hollywood types.

WHAT'S NEW? Don't miss Rock 'n Roller Coaster, a thrilling vertical corkscrew in what used to be the front corner of the parking area, and Fantasmic, Disney's best light show yet.

TIMING You can't quite do it all in a day, but it's going to be fun to try! Choose carefully.

EATERTAINMENT Disney's imaginative use of their movie themes makes eating here a memorable experience. Though you can sometimes just drop in, you should really make reservations way in advance (tel. 407/939–3463 or 407/WDW–DINE).

SHOPPERTOONITIES Here you'll find movie memorabilia, from autographs to animation cels. Prices range from "Wow, what a deal!" to "If you really want it honey, I guess we could sell the house."

PARADES AND FIREWORKS The Studios' parade, always a celebration of the latest animated flick, brings its characters to life. The nightly fireworks show has been replaced by **Fantasmic!**, Disney's most ambitious outdoor extravaganza yet, combining live action with pyrotechnics and amazing water effects in a 25-minute show that pits the main mouse against Disney's most celebrated villains. Here, the Imagineers have addressed my pet peeve at Epcot's IllumiNations (that you can't see the show) by creating a special 6,500-seat amphitheater behind Twilight Zone Tower of Terror, off Sunset Boulevard. Although every spectator has a perfect view, not everyone in the park will be able to get in. The show starts at

7:30 most nights; I predict a second show in future peak seasons. Check the daily schedule for times and arrive early to be sure you get a seat.

TV SHOW TAPINGS The **Production Information Window**, at the main entrance, dispenses information and tickets for shows that require an audience. But it's best to call ahead and schedule your time accordingly. (*See* my advice on attending tapings in Chapter 3.)

THE LAY OF THE LAND As you enter, you walk straight down Hollywood Boulevard. Sunset Boulevard is off to your right, Echo Lake to your left. Ahead, New York Street is roughly on the left, Mickey Avenue slightly to the right.

THE FAST TRACK My advice is to do all the attractions that involve walking first. The Magic of Animation, the Disney–MGM Studios Backlot Tour, and the *Honey, I Shrunk the Kids* adventure playground are much more enjoyable without sore feet. Plus, most people run for the rides right off the bat, so they're less crowded later in the day.

HOLLYWOOD BOULEVARD AND ECHO LAKE

A replica of Grauman's Chinese Theater, the scene of many Hollywood premieres in the old days, is straight ahead, dominating the park's skyline. On your left as you face the theater is a small lake, around which the park has re-created Hollywood's Echo Park, famous as a movie shoot location.

THE GREAT MOVIE RIDE The lobby of this Disney version of Hollywood's most famous landmark is full of memorabilia—most notably Dorothy's original ruby-red slippers. Inside, a tram takes you through scenes from the *Wizard of Oz, Mary Poppins,* and other great films, featuring perfectly detailed Audio-Animatronics replicas of screen idols such as John Wayne, Jimmy Cagney, and Edward G. Robinson. I won't spoil it for you except to say that it really *is* a great movie ride.

The Fast Track: The line here varies more than others, by turns nonexistent and very long. My advice: Never wait. If it looks like you'll have to, walk away and come back later.

Worth-It Rating ★★★★★

INDIANA JONES STUNT SPECTACULAR I was picked! Many volunteer, but few are chosen, and I was actually chosen to go down on the tarmac and play a bad guy in the redo of the exploding airplane scene in *Raiders of the Lost Ark.* I didn't do much, but what a view! This demonstration of stunt magic and acrobatics includes the race with the giant boulder from the movie. The wait is long and boring. Be patient.

Worth-It Rating ★★★★★

DISNEY'S DOUG, LIVE! AND ABC SOUND STUDIO ONE SATURDAY MORNING These two shows are similar to Universal's Hercules and Xena. But here, instead of a single experience, there are two separate attractions. Disney's Doug, Live! demonstrates visual effects in an interactive, audience-participation show in which several guests are picked for bit parts in the production. To show how the audio is created, **ABC Sound Studio** allows guests to try their hands at overdubbing. The results are a lot like badly dubbed foreign films, and they're always comical. Arrive early for both attractions, because a producer chooses the most enthusiastic spectators as participants before each show.

Worth-It Rating ★★★★ Add 1 if you know nothing about TV. Deduct 1 if you've been inside a studio.

STAR TOURS Okay, I keep saying it's a lot smaller than Universal's Back to the Future. But it's still a great ride. And it's not as rough. As the story goes, your shuttle to the moon of Endor is piloted by a rookie robot of monumental ineptitude—and that's where the thrills begin. The waiting area is part of the experience; it's pure *Star Wars,* a high-tech workshop littered with space junk and assorted 'droid parts. Plus, it's air-conditioned. Have your camera ready as you leave, because Chewbacca often hangs out in the exit area.

The Fast Track: Be on the lookout for a second line. When you first enter, you'll see a robot and spacecraft repair area with a steep ramp. Apparently, it's not obvious to everyone that there are usually two lines.

Worth-It Rating ★★★★★

ATAS HALL OF FAME Here, you'll find bronze busts of all of the Hall of Fame honorees of the Academy of Television Arts & Sciences. It's not too thrilling, but there's never a line.

BITES Every showbiz eatery worth its salt has caricatures on the walls, and why should the **Brown Derby** be an exception? The setting is stylish and faintly deco, and the presentations are impressive; the menu is straightforward American steaks, seafood, and pastas. Book ahead or come early. **Starring Rolls,** near the Brown Derby, invites you to ignore your diet. The 50's **Prime Time Café** makes you wonder: Is it dinner time or show time? A woman claiming to be your mother brings you meat loaf and insists that you eat your veggies, as tableside TVs play clips in beautiful black and white. My wife, Terrie, likes the huge peanut butter and jelly sandwiches. I have been seated unannounced, but it's best to come with reservations. **Hollywood & Vine Cafeteria**, next door, is your typical 1950s cafeteria—convenient and reasonably priced. Ricky, my son, loves the ribs. It's a big place, so lines are usually manageable. At the **ABC Commissary**, between the Great Movie Ride and the Sci-Fi Dine-In (*see below*), the food is nowhere near as bad as it is at the feeding troughs for which it is named. Look for burgers, fries, and chicken sandwiches.

On the shore of Echo Lake, you'll find **Dinosaur Gertie's Ice Creams of Extinction**, cleverly shaped like a dinosaur whose nose appears to smoke—courtesy of the cold air in the freezer. **Min & Bill's Dockside Diner** is another giant prop you just can't miss, an old gray junk freighter where you'll find snacks like yogurt, frozen fruit, and juices.

Backlot Express is another fast foodery. Or how about dinner in a '57 Chevy convertible served by a car-hop at the drive-in theater? The venue is the **Sci-Fi Dine-In Theater**, where tables are set up inside fake cars. Terrie goes for burgers, fries, and a shake. I love the seafood-topped pasta.

BUYS **Movieland Merchandise** and **Crossroads of the World** sell movie-theme souvenirs. Look to the left as you enter the park, and you'll see **Sid Cahuenga's One-of-a-Kind**, a virtual Hollywood museum. You might even see Sid, dressed in his safari outfit, rocking on the porch of his shop. The selection constantly changes—be on the lookout for private letters, autographed pictures, and personal keepsakes from some of the biggest stars of all time. Many of these items cost more than your entire vacation. Some cost more than my net worth. And others you can take home for a song (well, almost). Just to your right as you enter the park is **Oscar's Classic Car Souvenirs & Super Service**, a reproduction gas station. It's stocked with trinkets and toy-size classics like the famous '57 Chevys. **Darkroom**, nearby, handles photo supplies, rentals, and minor emergency repairs.

Heading down the Boulevard, you pass **Mickey's of Hollywood, Pluto's Toy Palace, Disney & Co,** and **LA Cinema Storage,** which sell Disney and Disney–MGM logo merchandise. At **Cover Story,** have your picture put on the cover of a fictitious magazine. **Celebrity 5 & 10,** a take-off on a vintage Woolworth store, fascinated my children as an example of how it was way back when Dad was a kid. **Keystone Clothiers** sells Beverly Hills-style outfits (with prices to match), all to give you that vintage Tinseltown look. **Lakeside News** stocks magazines—including showbiz titles.

Returning from Endor, you pass through **Endor Vendors,** which is loaded with *Star Wars* souvenirs and space toys. Ricky loves the **Indiana Jones Adventure Outpost** stand, which offers rubber snakes, variations on Indy's trademark hat, and more.

NEW YORK STREET

A technique called "forced perspective" lets filmmakers fake big-city skylines right on the lot. New York Street, used in *Dick Tracy,* is the perfect example.

JIM HENSON'S MUPPETVISION 4D This is a great show! Spectacularly silly, it's complete with exploding walls, rain from the ceiling, pies in the face, and other slapstick. You'll see all the Muppets you know and love along with a weird flying character created especially for this show.
The Fast Track: If you sit too close, you'll miss the best laughs (look for the two old guys in the box seats!).
Worth-It Rating ★★★★★

DISNEY'S THE HUNCHBACK OF NOTRE DAME—A MUSICAL ADVENTURE This is another of Disney's Broadway-quality live shows, performed at the Backlot Theatre and based on the animated feature of the same name. Spectacular special effects include a fly-in by Quasimodo.
The Fast Track: As for all live shows, check for showtimes and arrive 20–30 minutes early to get good seats.
Worth-It Rating ★★★★★

DISNEY'S TOY STORY PIZZA PLANET ARCADE Here you'll find pizza plus the latest in video games and other diversions, just like in the movie *Toy Story,* but tiny and underwhelming. I expected the claw machine to be full of aliens, as it was in the movie. It wasn't. Because of its pivotal role in the movie, I thought the pizza would be extra-special. It wasn't either.
Worth-It Rating ★★

HONEY, I SHRUNK THE KIDS MOVIE SET ADVENTURE This free-form playground is a great place to cool off on a hot day. You climb and slide on giant grass and trash, just like in the movie but with water squirting everywhere.
Worth-It Rating ★★★★ Add 1 if the line is short, as it often is.

BITES Mama Melrose's Ristorante Italiano fits the New York theme perfectly, with designer pizzas baked in a brick oven, pasta, steak, and seafood. You need reservations.

MICKEY AVENUE
AND THE ANIMATION COURTYARD

Here are Disney's working soundstages, where shows and/or films may be in progress.

BACKSTAGE PASS TO . . . Here you can check out props, costumes, sets, and filmmaking techniques from the latest Disney film.
Worth-It Rating ★★★

LIGHTS! CAMERA! ACTION! THEATER At this writing, this theater is showing "The Making of Armageddon." You may find something else, depending on what Disney is promoting when you visit. Regardless, you'll get a behind-the-scenes

look at the making of a major blockbuster, complete with film clips, star and director interviews, props, and costumes.
Worth-It Rating ★★★★

VOYAGE OF THE LITTLE MERMAID Ariel and Sebastian lead an all-starfish cast in this live adaptation of the Disney cartoon feature. Glowing, floaty, black-lit characters, a cool mist emanating from the ceiling, and a bubble machine make you feel truly sub-marine. Back in 1992, a college student named Leanza Cornett went from Ariel's throne to win the Miss America pageant. The stars are still that good.
Worth-It Rating ★★★★★

WALT DISNEY THEATER In this deliciously cool movie theater, you can sit down for half an hour and see made-for-the-Disney-Channel movies about Disney films.
Worth-It Rating ★★★

DISNEY–MGM STUDIOS BACKLOT TOUR Ironically, this is more like the original Universal Studios Hollywood tour than anything at Universal Studios Escape. It's part self-guided walking tour, part tram ride through production, wardrobe, props areas, a soundstage, and exhibit areas. You cruise a residential street lined with the homes of Beaver, the Golden Girls, and more—but there are no buildings behind the facades. In the Catastrophe Canyon section, a gas truck explodes and a flood threatens to deluge the tram, as at Universal's Earthquake: The Big One, but neither experience is as scary. However, the production is more impressive and gives you more in-depth explanation of the earthquake/explosion/flood effect than you get at Earthquake.

The Fast Track: Lines are long. Do it early or late. The wait may be shorter, and the scorching blast feels really miserable in the steamy late afternoon.
Worth-It Rating ★★★★★

THE MAGIC OF DISNEY ANIMATION You see artists working on future animated films on this self-guided multimedia tour of the artistic cornerstone of the empire. I was fascinated by the original multiplane camera, the Walt Disney invention that gives his early animation such unequaled realism. On display are original drawings and cels from Disney classics.
Worth-It Rating ★★★★★

THE AMERICAN FILM INSTITUTE SHOWCASE See actual costumes, props, and sets used in current hit movies. No lines.
Worth-It Rating ★★★

BITES The **Soundstage** food court—decorated with film artifacts—is the park's largest eatery, serving pizza and pasta, burgers, chicken, and salads. Character breakfasts and buffet lunches fill up fast, so book ahead. Above, you can sip (alcoholic) drinks high in the rigging at the **Catwalk Bar.** On a real movie set, such an activity would be high-risk. **Studio Catering**, across from the studio tour entrance, near the corner of Mickey Avenue and New York Street, has snacks.

BUYS **Under the Sea**, a souvenir stand just outside the Voyage of the Little Mermaid, is good for mermaid merchandise and movie memorabilia. Outside the Backstage Studio Tour and behind Catastrophe Canyon, **Studio Showcase** sells a variety of movie-theme gift items.

SUNSET BOULEVARD

TWILIGHT ZONE TOWER OF TERROR This is actually two rides, back to back. A Rod Serling double tells the attraction's story of an episode that never aired about a 1930s elevator crash caused by a lightning storm that shut down the Hollywood Hotel. Fascinating detail abounds, from the hotel's crumbling vine-covered facade to the dusty queue area inside, littered with the TV show's most memorable props. After you board an elevator in the mansion's spooky sub-cellar, a 13-story ride up with a quick view of the park is followed by a free-fall that includes a few seconds of actual weightlessness. Then, you repeat the elevator ride in the sequel. The long wait is definitely part of the experience.
Worth-It Rating ★★★★★

BEAUTY AND THE BEAST LIVE ON STAGE This amazing production at the Theater of the Stars was so well done that it was successfully adapted for Broadway.
Worth-It Rating ★★★★★

ROCK 'N ROLLER COASTER Next door to the Fantasmic amphitheater is this new indoor thrill ride. Climb aboard one of four 24-passenger limos for a breakneck cruise through Hollywood. Your jaunt includes three upside-down flips and a flight through the Hollywood sign.
Too new to rate.

BITES Sunset Ranch Market is a nifty bit of Disneyana, a re-creation of a place that Walt frequented in Anaheim around the time he bought the Disneyland property. You eat light fare outdoors on picnic tables. **Rosie (the Riveter's) Red Hot**

Dogs is on the same theme. Legend has it that Walt used to stop at the original for a hot dog when he visited Anaheim. You can, too—for chili dogs and chili.

BUYS The **Anaheim Produce Company** recalls the orange grove that became Disneyland. You'll find citrus to purchase. In the middle of Sunset Boulevard, **Once Upon a Time** sells merchandise from the classics. Near Hollywood Boulevard, **Legends of Hollywood** stocks books, posters, and videos of and about famous films. **Golden Age Souvenirs**, outside Superstar Television, sells goodies that recall the early days of TV. (Remember, at Disney, you're traveling through another dimension—a dimension not only of sight and sound but also of stuff.) At **Tower Hotel Gifts**, pick up a Serling for the den.

chapter 9

DISNEY'S ANIMAL KINGDOM

Take Exit 25B off I-4.

Off to a slow start, but it's rapidly getting better.

Back in 1997, a tree grew like crazy on 500 acres of the southwestern edge of Walt Disney World near Blizzard Beach and the All-Star Resorts. Over 14 stories high, the Tree of Life is the centerpiece of Disney's largest and most ambitious theme park yet, Disney's Animal Kingdom.

From Walt's *True Life Adventure* series to animated films featuring critters like Mickey Mouse, the Disney organization was built around our furry, feathered, finned, and fossilized friends. Disney's new Animal Kingdom, which is some five times the size of its Magic predecessor, was inspired by the late Uncle Walt's love for critters. Devoted to creatures real, imaginary, and extinct, it purports to be the world's largest zoo, and is said to be home to more than a thousand live animals along with Audio-Animatronics robots and classic Disney characters. Several live-animal expe-

Disney's Wild Animal Kingdom

KEY

🍴 Restaurants
🚻 Rest rooms

AFRICA

Tusker House

Harambe

Discovery River

First Aid

ASIA

SAFARI VILLAGE

CAMP MINNIE-MICKEY

OASIS

Guest Relations

Garden Gate Gifts

ATM

Lockers

Lockers

Entrance

Rainforest Café

DINOLAND U.S.A.

riences here put you face to face with animals who are restrained by barriers that are either invisible or cleverly disguised, so that you might experience the feeling of a journey into the wild.

Unfortunately, this park fails to live up to expectations because of two major shortcomings: while the rides and shows are good (and some are excellent), they are too few and far between to justify the expense of a theme-park day. Moreover, the main reason for the attraction's existence, the zoological park, misses the mark with a poorly executed safari ride and too few animal encounters.

Like all theme parks, this one is a collection of several lands on the animal theme. Hours of operation are more like a safari park's as well—from dawn until dark.

EATERTAINMENT Besides the famous Rain Forest Café (I love this place—see my review in Chapter 10) at the entrance, which starts serving breakfast at 6 AM, there are several good places to eat in Animal Kingdom. Two favorites are the Flame Tree Barbecue and Tusker House. Prices are reasonable, and the portions are ample.

SHOPPERTOONITIES Merchandise here is typical Disney—clothing, trinkets, lots of stuffed animals, and plenty of faux fur and leopard prints. Unique to the park is a large selection of imported arts-and-crafts items, including intricate African wood carvings, hand-made leather accessories, drums and other instruments, and folk art.

CHARACTER GREETING PAVILIONS Each Disney park features a special place to meet and greet the costumed characters, collect autographs, and pose for photos. Here, at Camp Minnie-Mickey, Minnie Mouse shares a garden spot with

Mickey and Goofy. Alternatively, look for Mickey at Mickey's State Park Pavilion, and for Winnie the Pooh, Tigger, and Eeyore at the Forest Pavilion. The Jungle Pavilion nearby hosts Rafiki, Timon, and Baloo. You'll find lots of meet-and-greet opportunities, with lines that are manageable—a must-see for kids.

Worth-It Rating ★★★★★

PARADES AND FIREWORKS The current parade is called "March of the ARTimals." Based on the fanciful animal drawings of Swiss artist Rolf Knie, it is a bigger-than-life, unduplicated, world-class production, not be missed.

TV SHOW TAPINGS TV shows often tape here. Check with Guest Relations when you visit.

THE LAY OF THE LAND As you enter, you will pass through the Oasis, cross the Discovery River, and enter Safari Village, the point of embarkation for the rest of the park. On your right is DinoLand U.S.A.; on your left is Camp Minnie-Mickey; and dead ahead is Africa.

THE FAST TRACK The best time to see animals is at sunrise. Most other savvy visitors know this. So, you'll hardly be alone, even at the crack of dawn. Head straight for the Kilimanjaro Safari Ride. See the animals waking up, then take in the rest of the park, as you please. Unlike almost any other park I can think of, there's not so much to do that you can't do most of it in a single day. In cool weather, when the safari can be taken at any time of day, follow my usual rule and stay to the left. Once you've taken the no-option route through the Oasis and Safari Village, begin the rest of your visit at Camp Minnie-Mickey, and do the park clockwise, stopping in Africa, Conservation Station, Asia, and Dinoland U.S.A. You'll hit the park's best ride, Countdown to Extinction, at the end of the day when lines should be shortest.

The first time we came was during the peak of summer, when the animals come out only at dawn and twilight. Our second visit was in January. We saw most of the animals, even in the middle of the day. A highlight was when a couple of large antelope stood in the road, refusing to allow our vehicle to pass, backing up several vehicles. Apparently, the animals have not been adequately prepped on the need for continuous traffic flow.

Don't use waterways as wishing wells. Coins change the chemistry of the water. Feeding the animals is also a big no-no.

At the "Outpost" you can get wheelchairs and strollers. Lines are much shorter than at similar places inside the park.

THE OASIS

You enter through a tropical garden with bright flowers, cool waterfalls, grottoes, and glades, where colorful creatures are abundant. Ducking under a thundering waterfall, you pass through a misty cloud to get to the **Rainforest Café,** an Audio-Animatronics dining adventure that is a sister to the amazing, like-named restaurant in Downtown Disney (*see* Chapter 10).

SAFARI VILLAGE

From the Oasis, a wooden bridge that spans the Discovery River brings you to this central crossroads. It's in the center of the Discovery River, and it's the starting point of all journeys through the Animal Kingdom. Dominating the village is the towering **Tree of Life**, nearly 200 feet above the ground and 50 feet around, with hundreds of hand-carved animals growing from its trunk. Most visitors take a few minutes to try to spot the carvings, which range from obvious to obscure.

IT'S TOUGH TO BE A BUG A look at life from a bug's-eye view from America's foremost computer genius, Steve Jobs, and Pixar, the people who brought you *Toy Story.* I won't spoil the surprises, but special effects allow you to feel and even smell the bugs. Some of it is not for the squeamish, but it's a hoot! *The Fast Track:* The line here varies more than many others, by turns nonexistent and very, very long. My advice: If the line is too long, walk away and come back later.
Worth-It Rating ★★★★★

DISCOVERY CRUISE This journey takes you past the dreaded Dragon Rocks, with views of steaming geysers, prehistoric beasts, and fantasy creatures en route. My son Ricky's reaction was, "Is that it?" I had to agree. It was sort of like Jungle Cruise at the Magic Kingdom, only without most of the action.
The Fast Track: If there's a line, I'd skip this ride altogether.
Worth-It Rating ★★

BITES **Flame Tree Barbecue** is our favorite, with low prices, great food, and good portions. My personal pick is the beef brisket sandwich. **Pizzafari**, near the path to Camp Minnie-Mickey, offers decent pizza and other quick fare, including some above-average sandwiches. Down the path, toward Camp Minnie-Mickey, you'll find **Forest Trail Funnel Cakes,** which sells (what else?) funnel cakes, as well as corn dogs on a stick. Just down the road is **Chip 'n Dale's**

Cookie Cabin, where the smell of big, yummy fresh-baked cookies will entice you.

BUYS Shopping abounds in Safari Village. **Island Mercantile** is the park's largest shop, with a selection that includes character jewelry and watches, safari suits and jungle-theme attire, toys and stuffed animals, and books and videos. Across the path, **Disney Outfitters** is an upscale clothing outlet with lots of leopard-print dresses, pantsuits, and hats. You'll also find the latest high-tech digital cameras. Artists stand ready to create hand-painted, one-of-a-kind, collectible character watches to your personal order. Just down the road, **Creature Comforts** specializes in children's clothing and toys. **Beastly Bazaar,** next to the Tree of Life, focuses on merchandise themed to *A Bug's Life* and the It's Tough To Be a Bug show next door. Here, embroiderers will put your name on hats and clothing.

DINOLAND U.S.A.

The new axiom among theme-park designers seems to be "You can't go wrong with dinosaurs."

BONEYARD A paleontological dig site-cum-playground where kids can search for buried "fossils," slide down the bones of T-Rex, and play with a triceratops and a 50-foot tall brachiosaurus.
Worth-It Rating ★★★ Add 2 for kids under 6.

COUNTDOWN TO EXTINCTION A multimedia simulator adventure using Audio-Animatronics and cars on tracks to complete the effect of total chaos. You'll journey 65 million years into the past to a smoky, primeval world where you'll barely escape a close encounter with dinosaurs, just before a comet collides with the earth, wiping out all of the dinosaurs forever. This state-of-the-art thrill ride is a little rough, but it's the best in the park.

The Fast Track: Skip it if you have any health or back problems.

Worth-It Rating ★★★★★

CRETACEOUS TRAIL On this considerably calmer nature walk you'll be reminded that many of today's plants and some animals have been with us a long time: Cycads, palms, ferns, and a few reptiles and amphibians have all survived from the age of the dinosaurs.

Worth-It Rating ★★★★★

BITES Restaurantosaurus has an all-you-can-eat breakfast buffet along with a character encounter featuring Donald, Mickey, Goofy, and Pluto. This is the only sit-down dining inside the park. Reserve ahead (tel. 407/WDW–DINE). At lunch and dinner, **Restaurantosaurus** is turned over to **McDonald's. Dino Diner** is the place to get those giant smoked turkey legs that are such a good deal. Two legs usually feed four of us, and we're big eaters. **Dinoland Snacks,** at the far end of Dinoland, is another **McDonald's.**

BUYS For fossils and lots of Dinosaur toys, head to **Chester and Hester's Dinosaur Treasures.**

CAMP MINNIE-MICKEY

Themed as a vacation camp in the Adirondack mountains, this is the Animal Kingdom's answer to the Magic Kingdom's Fantasyland.

THEATER IN THE WILD Shows may change, but at this writing they're showing "Journey Into Jungle Book," a musical production based on the Disney cartoon adaptation of the Rudyard Kipling classic. The rowdy and rousing rendition does justice to the material.
Worth-It Rating ★★★★★

FESTIVAL OF THE LION KING This abbreviated version of the Broadway musical hit is awesome, with colorful costumes, spectacular scenery and fabulous song and dance. The only drawback is the pavilion in which the show is presented—a tent that was hot, muggy, and full of mosquitoes when we were there.
Worth-It Rating ★★★★ Add 1 in cooler weather.

COLORS OF THE WIND Characters from the animated hit *Pocahontas* headline an educational and informative live show that features interaction with critters who variously hop, fly, and slither.
Worth-It Rating ★★★★

AFRICA

At the town of Harambe, on the edge of the African savannah, herds of zebras, giraffes, lions, and elephants, including several endangered African species, roam a landscape of rich forests, tropical rivers, and wide open plains.

KILIMANJARO SAFARI Set in the African wilderness during monsoon season, your safari encounters a band of nasty poachers in the midst of evil doings. You'll race over washed-out roads and through landslides and flash floods before finally crossing a crocodile-infested river by way of a collapsing bridge. The hard fiberglass seats make the ride unnecessarily rough.
The Fast Track: Again, the best time to see animals is at dawn or dusk (I recommend dawn).
Worth-It Rating ★★★★ Minus 2 if you go at midday.

PANGANI FOREST EXPLORATION TRAIL Another nature walk, this one takes you through the habitat of the lowland gorilla. Underwater windows in a tank-cum-lagoon give you a unique view of bathing hippos. The trail also steers you into a walk-through aviary filled with exotic birds. Ricky and my wife, Terrie, called this the highlight of their trip into the Animal Kingdom.
Worth-It Rating ★★★★★

WILDLIFE EXPRESS TO CONSERVATION STATION Cross the African savannah to the Conservation Station and the Animal Kingdom infirmary, where you'll meet trainers and experts in an interactive and educational experience that focuses on the battle against extinction. A must if you love animals—after all, they're what it's all about.
Worth-It Rating ★★★★★

BITES In Harambe the **Tusker House Restaurant** serves full-size meals of fried or rotisserie chicken, a hearty beef stew in a bread bowl, and some very healthy pocket-bread veggie sandwiches, all in a casual atmosphere. Nearby is another favorite, **Tamu-Tamu,** where you can get a large and yummy hot-fudge or strawberry sundae. In Harambe's square, **Dawa Bar** offers a selection of cool cocktails served to the strains of an African folk band. **Kusafiri Coffee Shop and Bakery** serves cappuccino, espresso, and some nice fat pastries. **Harambe Fruit Market** has fresh fruits, juices, and other soft drinks.

BUYS In Harambe, **Mambasa Market/Ziwani Traders** sells safari apparel and a large collection of hand-carved African folk art. **Duka La Filmu** is a little stand with Kodak film and cameras, as well as some small items such as autograph books and rain ponchos. At the back of Conservation Station, **Out of the Wild** is a small shop that focuses on the plight of endangered species and habitats with lifelike animal figures, books, T-shirts, and other conservation-theme items.

ASIA

Only partially complete at this writing, Asia promises to expand and improve the park with the addition of important new animals and a thrilling new ride—the Kali River Rapids.

FLIGHTS OF WONDER This "birds of prey" show features trained and performing hawks and other predators, including the giant Eurasian owl-hawk, in free flight over the park. The trainers narrate a true-life adventure show that is educational, informative, and sometimes amazing.
Worth-It Rating ★★★★★

MAHARAJAH JUNGLE TREK This walking tour of the Anandapur Royal Forest and hunting lodge, stocked with hundreds of colorful exotic birds and plants, will put you face to face with tigers and such exotic creatures as the giant Komodo dragon.

Too new to rate.

KALI RIVER RAPIDS This ride is similar to the Congo River Rapids at Busch Gardens. You'll board an eight-passenger tube craft and plunge through raging rapids. Expect to get thoroughly soaked—a welcome experience on a hot Florida day. I can't rate it, because it hasn't been built yet, but from the plans, I'd give it two thumbs up!

Too new to rate.

BITES **Drinkwallah** is a cola stand in a charming dilapidated outpost. Nearby **Anapour Ice Cream** sells cold treats like refreshing fruit smoothies and ice cream floats.

chapter 10

DOWNTOWN DISNEY

From I–4, take Exit 26, marked for Route 536. Head on Epcot Center Drive to Buena Vista Drive, then turn right. (Although you'll drive a longer distance than if you come via Exit 27, marked for Route 535, you'll actually spend less time, because there's so much more traffic on 535.)

You can't do everything here in Orlando, but if Downtown Disney is one of your choices, you won't regret it!

Downtown Disney, now a destination attraction in its own right, is the complex made up of the Disney attractions in the Lake Buena Vista area between Routes 535 and 536. These include longtime favorites Disney Village Marketplace and Pleasure Island as well as the former Hotel Plaza, plus a new and totally spectacular addition to Disney's nightlife and shopping scene— the West Side.

There must be a bunch of reasons for so many people to come here, and there are! From fine dining to fast food, from fine art to knickknacks, there's something for everyone, every age, and every taste.

TIMING Come during the day for lunch and some leisurely shopping, or come at sundown to party until 2 AM.

THE LAY OF THE LAND Downtown Disney runs parallel to I-4 between Route 535 on the north and Route 536 on the south. If you enter as I suggest, from the south via Route 536, you'll take Exit 26B, marked for Epcot, off I-4, then turn north on Buena Vista Drive. The first left turnoff you come to is for Disney's West Side; then, also on your left, are turns for Pleasure Island and the Marketplace, near Route 535.

THE FAST TRACK This enormous complex is currently suffering from too much success. Traffic is terrible! On the last several trips, I have allowed myself an extra half hour for traffic, parking, and walking from a distant parking spot, and it has never been enough! My favorite end-run, at this writing, is outlined above. I avoid much chaos this way. As you'll soon see for yourself, the Disney traffic planners have their own ideas about how you should get around and have set up the signs to direct you to Route 535, which feeds you right into a snarl that includes the entrance to Hotel Plaza. Still, even though their signs don't always tell you that Route 536 takes you to Downtown Disney, they have done a good job marking the road itself.

Once inside, crowds flow counterclockwise, so once again, my advice is to go against the flow.

Here are some other tips:

- Though many places don't require reservations, "priority seating" is often available. (This is something like a reservation—the restaurant won't have a table waiting, but your name will go to the top of the list when you arrive.) Go for priority seating wherever you can. You'll be competing with thousands of others for each pricey experience (and remember, when your vacation is concerned, your time is money, too), so take any advantage you can get.

- Come early—traffic peaks in the complex at around 8 PM, so the earlier you arrive the better your chance to get ahead of the mob.
- Don't count on valet parking. Depending on where you're going, you may be able to park closer by looking for a regular spot. And on my last trip, lines of cars waiting for attendants were backed up worse than the traffic to get into the lots. Often, the only valet parking is at one end of the complex or the other.
- If you're coming from elsewhere on Disney property, you may want to leave your car and use complimentary Disney transportation—it's faster and easier, and gets you closer. And you'll appreciate a bus or boat even more when you're leaving.
- If you're staying in WDW hotels, remember that you can have purchases made in the shops delivered directly to your room—see, you *can* go clubbing and shopping in a single night.

The West Side

This complex of clubs, concert halls, and restaurants with a scattering of shops is the biggest and best part of Downtown Disney. Although the pay-as-you-go policy can make the experience pricey, everything you find is brand-spanking-new and state-of-the-art, and should be high enough in quality to justify your outlay (although many of these attractions were not sufficiently complete at the time of this writing for me to rate them).

CIRQUE DU SOLEIL Forget the term circus—it won't help you envision this acrobatic tour de force from Montréal's famed Circus of the Sun. There are no animal acts in this show; instead, high flyers and highly skilled acrobats perform to sizzling music in a state-of-the-art theater under a brightly colored, extravagantly illuminated circus tent. *$56.50 general, $42.20 ages 3–9, plus tax. Seats may be reserved by calling 407/939–7600.*
Worth-It Rating ★★★★★

HOUSE OF BLUES This theme restaurant from Dan Aykroyd, Jim Belushi, and pals may be the biggest and best of all the theme restaurants owned by celebrities—and there are several around town. Its multilevel concert hall regularly hosts the big names in blues, soul, and rock. The food served here and in an adjacent restaurant is Cajun-style with plenty of barbecue and carbohydrates, and overly generous desserts. Jambalaya, étouffée, gumbo, and bread pudding are the specialties. Walls are covered from floor to ceiling with American folk art. On Sunday, the main event is the all-you-can-eat gospel brunch, an experience unduplicated in our area that is definitely a Worth-It. Advance tickets are usually required along with a specific seating time. *Tel. 407/934–2583. Entrées $8.50–$13.*
Worth-It Rating ★★★★★

DISNEYQUEST This huge, high-tech fun center is the prototype for a series of mini–Disney Worlds coming soon to a city near you. Entering its Ventureport, the gateway to the complex, brings you to four virtual worlds. The Explore

Zone takes you riding raging rapids, visiting ancient lands, and speeding through outer space. The Score Zone pits you against superheroes in battles of skill and daring. The Create Zone is your own private Imagineering studio, where you can create art and concoct special effects. And in the Replay Zone, billed as a "Carnival on the Moon," classic games meet outer space in a wacky send-up of the old-time midway. *Tel. 407/828–4600. $25 general, $20 for children ages 3–9, children under 3 free.*
Worth-It Rating ★★★

VIRGIN MEGASTORE In its three stories, the ultimate multimedia superstore from tycoon Richard Branson houses over 200,000 titles of music, video, and printed products, 300 listening booths, 20 movie preview stations, an indoor-outdoor café, a video wall, a satellite-uplinked TV studio, and, above the entrance, an elevated stage that regularly hosts some of the biggest names in entertainment and where we once saw our favorite band, Sister Hazel. *Tel. 407/828–0222.*
Worth-It Rating ★★★★★

WOLFGANG PUCK CAFE Okay, Orlando is full of restaurants owned by stars, but where do the stars eat? In Hollywood, one of their favorites is Spago, owned by restaurateur Wolfgang Puck. Here, Puck is producing fast food at surprisingly reasonable prices—creative pizzas, grilled fish, and vegetable spring rolls. Plus, there's a sushi bar and, upstairs, a really good fancy restaurant with ambitious cuisine. Celebrity spotting: I saw Kathy Lee Gifford here. I understand it's one of her favorites. Priority seating is available and is a good idea for dinner. *Tel. 407/939–9653. Entrées $16–$20.*
Worth-It Rating ★★★★★ +

GUITAR GALLERY BY GEORGE'S MUSIC A local music store, George's Music takes its place on the world stage in this double-decker showcase of music accessories, books, clothing, and learn-an-instrument packages. Many of the collectible guitars on display are replicas of instruments that have been owned and played by the world's most famous practitioners. Although they range in price from a few dollars to tens of thousands, it costs you nothing to gawk at the dazzling stainless steel surroundings, spectacular neon, and startling props like the 30-foot-high guitar strummed by an animated hand. *Tel. 407/352–8000.*
Worth-It Rating ★★★★★

BONGOS CUBAN CAFÉ When you count restaurant-owning stars, don't overlook Gloria Estefan and her producer husband, Emilio. Inside the sky-high pineapple dominating the Downtown Disney skyline, they preside over a set that evokes the famous Copacabana. You almost expect to see Desi Arnaz and Xaviar Cugat as you sway to the Latin music they loved on the expansive dance floor. The cuisine is every bit as Latin as the live nightly entertainment, and the Cuban coffee as strong as nearby NASA's shuttle fuel. Unfortunately, the food is below average, the portions are small, and the prices are high. Priority seating is available. *Tel. 407/828–0999. Entrées $16–$20.*
Worth-It Rating ★★★

AMC 24 THEATER COMPLEX Billed as the largest theater complex in the Southeast, this has 24 theaters and over 6,000 seats. There's Sony Digital Sound throughout; seating is plush and, in 18 theaters, it's terraced and arranged stadium style, with 6 feet of leg room and love seats for two. Two theaters are huge and balconied. It's a great place to catch a movie you'd want to see anyway. *For showtimes and info, call Teleticket at tel. 407/298–4488.*

Worth-It Rating ★★★★★

PLANET HOLLYWOOD Inside the globe that dominates the Downtown Disney scene, I ate Thai shrimp, and my son, Ricky, the rib expert, gave a thumbs-up to the generous portion of extra-tender St. Louis-style BBQ. Four jam-packed levels display the world's largest and most amazing collection of Hollywood costumes, props, art, and memorabilia. The multimedia show on several giant screens around the room is newsreel, movie trailer, home video, and corporate hype rolled into one spectacular bit of razzle-dazzle. The experience is overpoweringly intense. Come early and plan to wait, and wait, and wait. *Tel. 407/827–7827. Entrées $10–$15.*

Worth-It Rating ★★★★★

DISNEY'S CANDY CAULDRON Snow White's nemesis, the Wicked Queen, and her many costumed helpers, invite you to step into their delightfully dark, dank dungeon to take a bite of the candy apple. While you're on the premises, try the fresh fudge, the cotton candy, or any of the other confections that are made right before your watering mouth.

Worth-It Rating ★★★

FORTY THIRST STREET Even when you just stop for coffee or juice in Downtown Disney, it's a total sensory experience. This coffee bar-gone-fantastic includes a multiscreen laser light show with surround sound and fiber optics everywhere. Your coffee is made from freshly ground beans, roasted before your eyes.

Worth-It Rating ★★★

CELEBRITY EYEWORKS STUDIO Beneath your feet is a replica of Hollywood's Walk of Fame. Overhead, a video crew on a catwalk is shooting for an upcoming production. Check the monitor—you're the star! In Downtown Disney, the local frame shop is like that. The eyeware is trendy, from glasses to shades, and displayed amid photos of celebs in glasses—Hollywood's greatest "spectacles!"
Worth-It Rating ★★★

DAVID COPPERFIELD'S MAGIC UNDERGROUND The celebrated magician, escape artist, and showman has assembled a giant collection of magic tricks and illusions, exotic gifts, and exclusive signature clothing for sale to both beginning magicians and expert practitioners of the art of hocus-pocus.
    Too new to rate.

HOYPOLOI The waterfalls, wind chimes, knickknacks, and other decorative items here will all give you good *feng shui* (an environment in harmony with nature shaped by a talked-about Chinese discipline).
Worth-It Rating ★★★★

MAGNETRON A store created just for people who collect refrigerator magnets? Here is the world's largest and most extensive collection of "attractive" gifts, souvenirs, and other items that do more than just hang around.
Worth-It Rating ★★★★★

SOSA FAMILY CIGARS Although government is fighting tobacco in all its forms, cigar smoking is newly fashionable. My family remains opposed, so I will not rate this collection of cigars, humidors, and smoking accessories from a famous name in tobacco.

STARABILIAS If you've been dying to re-create that Cracker Barrel look in your own den, make a beeline for this store where you'll find a jumble of old metal advertising signs and other collectibles ranging from autographs to nickel Coke machines. Everything is for sale, including the life-size Colonel Sanders I saw on my last visit, but it's fun just to browse.
Worth-It Rating ★★★★★

WILDHORSE STORE You can't miss this retail arm of the nearby Wild Horse Saloon, with it's wild, wild Western display of cowboy hats, boots, belts, leather clothing and accesories, and everything else for the upscale cowpoke, whether urban, suburban, or even authentic. I found no bargains here, but there is a worthy selection of fine Western wear.
Worth-It Rating ★★★

MIDWAY GAMES Pleasure Island's version of the old carnival midway with all of those wonderful games of chance that I never can win. Some people do, however, and walk out with giant stuffed animals (unless, as at the carnival, they're shills).
Worth-It Rating ★★★

Pleasure Island

Pleasure Island is essentially a handful of nightclubs with a single, joint admission price and fairly uniform drink prices. Whether or not you enjoy any given club depends on your own tastes—so I've just given you one overall rating for the whole shebang. Is it worth your time and money? Admission is just under $20, and drinks start at around $3 for domestic beers, with specialty mixed drinks in the $10-and-up range, about the same as at other nightlife attractions. You can save money by getting your evening's pass included in a Disney length-of-stay pass or by asking for discount tickets—sometimes available at Disney restaurants and hotels. Regardless, if a nightlife attraction is what you're looking for, this one is first-class. Call 407/934–7781 for any of the following club schedules.

Once you've bought the general admission ticket, you can come and go as you wish, entering and leaving any of the clubs at will.

Note that Portobello, Fulton's, and the AMC Theaters are open to the public, without the Pleasure Island cover charge.

WEST END STAGE Every night at midnight, the folks at Pleasure Island remind you that tomorrow is the first day of the rest of your life with a New Year's celebration complete with fireworks. Major concert artists, from country, rock, and pop to R&B, jazz, and rap, also perform. *Call 407/824–9311 for schedules.*

THE BET SOUNDSTAGE Black Entertainment Network operates this club featuring R&B, soul, jazz, blues, rap, and hip-hop. Here, you won't forget that African-American entertainers like Chuck Berry and Little Richard also invented that thing called rock and roll.

COMEDY WAREHOUSE The place to catch stand-up and improv from house comics and the occasional national performer. The place is usually packed, and there are no reservations. So if this is your choice, start your evening here. Personally, the last time I was here, I did not feel that the comedy was worth the wait.

8TRAX Remember John Travolta as Tony Manero in *Saturday Night Fever?* You'll see lots of guys doing those steps over the same pulsating, translucent rainbow dance floor. A too-loud sound system completes the totally tacky effect.

MANNEQUINS DANCE PALACE The biggest draw on the island features contemporary music with a state-of-art sound and video setup, a live DJ, professional dancers, and a dazzling light show. The dance floor revolves, and the young people who generally fill the place are a show of their own.

ADVENTURERS CLUB I say, old chap, this place simply defies simple description. In one of its spooky rooms, primitive masks suddenly start to talk; in the salon, adventurers regale guests with tall tales. If you're like me, you'll enjoy the chance to jump in and play with the actors (one night I plan to dress up and pretend I'm one of them). If you're like my wife, Terrie, you'll sit back, sip your drink, and watch an old man make a fool of himself. A hoot!

ROCK & ROLL BEACH CLUB This three-story surf bar must have been designed by someone who went to the old Ocean Pier in Daytona to see the Beach Boys with me. When you climb the funky old stairs, you'll hear music that's just like you remember it, too—early garage-band. The night isn't complete without a rousing sing-along to "Louie, Louie"! Anybody for "Wild Thing"?

PLEASURE ISLAND JAZZ COMPANY This place has all that jazz, from swing to fusion, from New Orleans to experimental improv, courtesy of name musicians and talented locals. The room is laid-back and comfortable, evoking the spirit of Thelonius Monk.

WILD HORSE SALOON Ricky won't miss the Fireworks Factory, the restaurant that occupied this space, where he burned his mouth so badly on Dad's hot sauce that he couldn't eat any dinner. Its replacement is from Chicago's Levy Restaurants and the Nashville Network (TNN). TNN is providing the country-music talent, Levy the great barbecue. There's also a country-and-western store.

The Marketplace at Downtown Disney

★★★★★

Previously known as Disney Village Marketplace, Walt Disney World Shopping Village, and a handful of other names, this is the oldest part of Downtown Disney, with a wide selection of shopping and dining.

FULTON'S CRAB HOUSE This replica of a paddle-wheel riverboat, the former *Empress Lilly,* is now an excellent seafood restaurant that serves some of the best crab cakes anywhere. There is also a daily character breakfast. *Tel. 407/WDW–DINE. Entrées $15–$21.*

PORTOBELLO YACHT CLUB This sleek, stylish restaurant serves pasta, chicken, veal, and other Northern Italian specialties we've always enjoyed. Priority seating available. *Tel. 407/934–8888. Entrées $15–$25.*

RAINFOREST CAFÉ As you enter from the West Side, it's hard to miss the 65-foot active volcano that marks the entrance to this restaurant-store-attraction. Outside, you may encounter an animal trainer introducing a cockateel to visitors. Inside, you can wander more or less freely; it's a total-immersion experience, complete with robotic animals and special effects including a "thunderstorm" (every 20 minutes—actually only a refreshing mist). There's an eternal line for a table, where the patient chow down on traditional steaks as well as exotic dishes like blackened meatloaf, which is absolutely nothing like anything Mama used to make. Exotic drinks and desserts are both enormous and excellent. *Tel. 407/827–8500. Entrées $10–$15.*

THE ART OF DISNEY Disney animation art and collectibles have skyrocketed in value over the years. So they're not only excellent as decoration but may be good investments as well.

2R'S READING & RITING This Disney book store sells current best-sellers, children's books, reading accessories, some toys, and drinks from the now-obligatory cappuccino bar.

TEAM MICKEY'S ATHLETIC CLUB Here you'll find sports clothing and equipment with the Team Mickey and other college and pro-club logos, along with sports memorabilia of all kinds.

WOLFGANG PUCK CAFÉ Sharing the building with Team Mickey is the second of Puck's two Downtown Disney locations (*see above*). *Tel. 407/938–9653. Entrées $10–$30.*

RESORTWEAR UNLIMITED This is the place to find Lancôme beauty products, designer casual wear, and bathing attire for the country-club crowd.

AUTHENTIC ALL-STAR GEAR The retail end of the All-Star Café, the celebrity sports-theme restaurant at Disney's Wide World of Sports, sells sports gear from boxer shorts to hockey pucks, plus tons of T-shirts.

CAP'N JACK'S OYSTER BAR The nautical setting and lagoon view are pleasant but, considering how casual it all is, prices may be a bit high, even for the excellent chowder, fine jumbo shrimp cocktail, and fabulously pink strawberry margaritas.

SUMMER SANDS Check out the straw hats and canvas bags, summery clothing and jewelry, and shades, not to mention the loads of wonderfully tacky Floridiana.

GOURMET PANTRY It's an eatery on one side, a retail store on the other, both packed with delectable delights: deli goodies, wines, kitchen gadgets, cookbooks, and culinary aids. A cornucopia of kitchen kitsch!

HARRINGTON BAY CLOTHIERS Aw, shucks, you left your favorite Ralph Lauren outfit at home! Tell Buffy not to worry! You can pick up a replacement here.

TOYS FANTASTIC When we saw this all-Mattel store, my daughter, Tiffany, made a beeline for the Barbies—the selection was bountiful. (Not so that of the boys' toys.)

DISNEY'S DAYS OF CHRISTMAS A year-round Christmas store with the Disney characters (what else?) on ornaments.

GHIRARDELLI SODA FOUNTAIN & CHOCOLATE SHOP You'll find chocolates, ice cream, and soda-fountain specialties at this branch of San Francisco's famous chocoholic fantasy. Bring your sweet tooth.

EUROSPAIN Crystal is cut and glass is blown before your eyes here. The results are for sale, along with other art in glass, ceramics, jewelry, and European collectibles. Although most items are fairly pricey, some are surprisingly reasonable.

DISCOVER Learning toys, books and accessories, scientific stuff, environmentally aware animal toys, and other imagination-sparking items for kids of all ages keep company with a large selection of Disney character items in the same vein. It's hard not to like a place like this.

WORLD OF DISNEY The world's largest Disney store is actually 12 huge boutiques filled with everything Disney. Stuffed animals? There are thousands, along with jewelry, books, videos, toys, clothing, even intimate apparel—Minnie's Secret, anyone? The selection is awesome.

LEGO IMAGINATION CENTER At this Lego superstore—one of only two in the entire world at this writing—the awesome Lego structures on display include an amazing interactive outdoor playground and a 30-foot LEGO sea serpent. The frequent demonstrations of Lego art are fascinating. For Lego fans, this is a must-see.

STUDIO M A photo-op with the world's most famous mouse, plus Mickey photos and frames.

MARKETPLACE ACTIVITIES

BOATIN' AND FISHIN' While shopaholics search out the perfect Mickey golf balls, the rest of us rent the little sporty two-person boats known as Water Sprites at **Cap'n Jack's Marina.** Although you can rent them on many Disney waters, this marina is the most convenient place to rent 'em if you're staying off-property. (Note: You must be 14 to drive.) The marina is also a departure point for guided fishing trips in search of Florida's famous largemouth bass. And you can rent cane poles for angling off the dock—you'll catch shiners and maybe a bass. All fishing is catch-and-release only. *Tel. 407/828–2461.*

FUN, FOUNTAINS, AND SAND Water jumping out of the sidewalk from the computerized fountains here cools young and old alike on hot Florida days. You're in Disney—so have some fun, scream, and get wet! Nearby, right by the waterfront, is **Sand Street Station**, a giant sandbox and playground with a kids' train ride, a cute little diversion on a busy Disney day. Or just kick back at secluded **Sunset Cove** with a beach chair and an ice-cold drink; it's also by the water.

MCDONALD'S McDonald's at Disney—it was inevitable. What, you didn't come all this way for a Big Mac? Near Lego and Studio M.

SHOWS For years we have come to the **Dock Stage** for the annual Christmas shows. There are also seasonal concerts and special shows of all kinds, some of them excellent. *Check with Guest Services at 407/824–4321.*

chapter 11

UNIVERSAL'S CITYWALK

Follow the directions to Universal Studios Escape given in Chapter 3. From the parking garage a moving sidewalk transports you to CityWalk's central plaza.

One of the premier dining and nightlife areas in the world.

This giant entertainment complex, which looks something like a modern baseball stadium except with buildings where the seating would be, is the hub of the new Universal Studios Escape. All visitors enter through CityWalk, on their way to either Universal Studios Florida or Universal's Islands of Adventure. It's home to a dozen high-profile theme clubs and restaurants, with their attached shops—each one a separate attraction in its own right, with a separate admission. A large waterway through City-Walk's center is spanned by two bridges and traversed by boats and Venetian-style gondolas. The gigantic new Hard Rock Live Orlando concert venue, a spectacular re-creation of Rome's Colosseum, dominates the eastern shore of the waterway.

TIMING Everything is open daily. You can come by day for shopping and have a meal in one of the clubs or wait until dark for the nightlife and do your shopping between music stops. Count on spending up to four or five hours.

THE FAST TRACK If you plan to go at night, call 407/363–8000 to find out what's on and make your reservations as far ahead as possible.

THE LAY OF THE LAND Individual destinations here are arranged in a semicircle. Entries below are arranged in geographic order, starting on the left as you get off of the moving sidewalk and heading clockwise through the complex.

THE SCENE

NASCAR CAFÉ This details the racing theme right down to the pit-crew uniforms of the wait staff, the seating in rows of gleaming race cars, and the eating utensils, which look like mechanic's tools. So in some ways, it is similar to I-Drive's Race Rock, one of our family favorites. However, this place is much larger, with two levels, and it is NASCAR-sanctioned. A video wall shows clips, and you see memorabilia and rare NASCAR artifacts and collectibles at every turn. In the kids' arcade, all the games are based on NASCAR themes. To eat? Heaps of barbecue, fried chicken, and good ol' American meat and potatoes. When races are in town at Disney's Walt Disney World Speedway, count on catching NASCAR legends when they stop in to grab a bite and sign autographs.

UNIVERSAL CITY CINEPLEX Want to catch a movie? Catch this cutting-edge showcase for the newest films with giant screens, high-fidelity surround sound, and stadium seating. The 16-screen, 5,000-seat complex also houses several eateries, cafés, and shops.

MOTOWN CAFE The "Temptations" and the "Supremes"—two house groups faithfully commemorating the classic stars—take turns performing onstage at this club inspired by the music of the Detroit recording label that gave us those legendary acts as well as the Jackson Five, the Four Tops, and almost every other seminal R&B entertainer of the last 30 years. The menu offers soul food and such, including sweet-potato fries, meat loaf, and a range of large and gooey desserts. Photos, life-size statues, and memorabilia from some of Motown's most popular artists are on display. The obligatory on-premises shop sells everything from souvenir T-shirts to gold records and collectible 45s from Motown's golden era, the 1960s.

BOB MARLEY—A TRIBUTE TO FREEDOM In an authentic replica of reggae star Bob Marley's own Jamaican house and garden, you get a chance to soak up Jamaican culture along with Jamaica's food, spirits, and music. Marley's extended musical family, including his singer/songwriter son, Ziggy, are all involved in the operation and occasionally stop by to entertain. You can try Jamaica's national dish, curried goat, or go for more familiar entrées, along with island beers and rums.

PAT O'BRIEN'S The landmark New Orleans speakeasy, which calls itself the birthplace of dueling pianos as entertainment, is also the birthplace of the Hurricane—one of the world's most famous specialty drinks and the granddaddy of all specialty drinks. CityWalk's Pat O'Brien's has everything you find in the New Orleans original, right down to the fabled flaming fountain—a spectacle of fire and water.

JIMMY BUFFETT'S MARGARITAVILLE Most of the renowned Florida troubadour's best material concerns food and drink, so it's no wonder that he is now inviting parrotheads (as his fans call themselves) and the rest of us to have a "cheeseburger in paradise" or simply to "waste away again in Margaritaville." Remember the line, "Smell of shrimp, they're beginning to boil?" You can expect plenty of such Key West specialties, including several dishes based on native conch, and Key lime pie colored the proper yellow (no, it's not supposed to be green). Late nights at CityWalk's Margaritaville, you may be able to catch performances by the best of Florida's many guitar-strumming Buffett impersonators and even, on occasion, by the "Son of a Son of a Sailor" himself.

CITYJAZZ The centerpiece of a hotbed of jazz is an acoustically perfect, state-of-the-art concert hall, designed for jazz. Flanking the hall on one side is *Down Beat* magazine's Hall of Fame, where jazz legends, living and otherwise, have been inducted into immortality amidst the world's largest collection of jazz memorabilia, under the supervision of the definitive authorities, the editors of *Down Beat*. In the Thelonius Monk Institute of Jazz, opposite the Hall of Fame, jazz greats train up-and-comers and guests are invited to listen.

EMERIL'S RESTAURANT ORLANDO "BAM!" Here, fans of wacky TV Food Network chef Emeril Lagasse, a *Good Morning America* regular, will recognize that trademark exclamation and the high-energy hubbub in the open kitchen of the master chef's only venture outside New Orleans. Even if you don't know Lagasse from his show, you may want to sample what he calls his "kicky cuisine"—slightly crazed dishes like pistachio-orange-crusted scallops.

HARD ROCK CAFÉ As large as the famous giant guitar-shape building at Universal Studios was, it was still not big enough to house the enormous crowds drawn. So the HRC has moved to an even larger home, appropriately modeled after Rome's Colosseum. This is the most acoustically perfect concert hall I've ever been in. Although no slaves or gladiators are on hand, there is no shortage of rock memorabilia, Save the Planet T-shirts, and other souvenirs, not to mention the trademark pig sandwich—the best pulled-barbecue anywhere.

HARD ROCK LIVE ORLANDO Not to be outdone by House of Blues, Wild Horse Saloon, and other theme-joints-come-lately, the original celebrity restaurant has created a concert hall. The permanent home for its nationally televised *Hard Rock Live* television show, it features rock veterans and up-and-coming stars in nightly concerts. For schedules, call 407/351–7625.

chapter 12

MORE EATERTAINMENT

Tooth Picks, Plus a Little Night Music

The world's number one vacation destination will never lack places to eat and make merry. But beware: With over 40 million visitors each year, who needs repeat business? That's why you have me around. I describe a few of my favorites below. Unless otherwise noted, all accept major credit cards and are open daily. The range of prices listed at the end of each review is for dinner entrées.

MY SHORT LIST

BOSTON LOBSTER FEAST This is Orlando's best deal on a meal! It is also my favorite buffet anywhere! All-you-can-eat steamed lobster with hot butter is the Maine attraction at this restaurant adjoining the Florida Mall, along with crab, shrimp, oysters, clams, and fresh fish. I love the calamari salad, the lobster bisque, and the New England clam chowder. (Plenty for landlubbers, too, including a fine London broil.) Salads and tasty desserts round out the deal. It's at the intersection of Sand Lake Road and Orange Blossom Trail. *8204 Crystal Clear La., Orlando, tel. 407/438–0607. $24.95 adults, $15.95 children under 12 for the buffet; entrées $9.95– $18.95. No reservations.*

OUTBACK RESTAURANT AT WYNDHAM PALACE By far the best family dining on Disney property is at the Wyndham Palace, the premier resort at Downtown Disney. The Outback—*not* part of the national chain—comes complete with a stuffed crocodile in a rushing stream, aboriginal weapons and costumes on the walls, a dugout canoe hanging from the ceiling, and a general out-in-the-wild feel. A superb steak will be prepared before your eyes on the "barbee" (Aussie for barbecue), or you could go for seafood, most notably the enormous, excellent, and reasonably priced lobster (around $10 a pound). *1900 Buena Vista Dr., Lake Buena Vista, tel. 407/827– 2727. Entrées $13–$32.*

PONDEROSA GRAND BUFFET I rate this as Orlando's absolute best family buffet. True, Ponderosa is a national chain, but I've been all over the country and I've never seen any like the Ponderosas here. They're the cleanest and best anywhere, colorfully decorated and with a fabulous, attractively presented selection of over 100 fresh, tasty, all-American and Americanized dishes, both hot and cold, at every meal. *Orlando: 5535 S. Kirkman Rd., tel. 407/345–0200; 6362 International Dr., tel. 407/352–9343; 8510 International Dr., tel. 407/354–1477; and 14407 International Dr., tel. 407/238–2526.*

Kissimmee: 7598 W. Irlo Bronson Memorial Hwy., tel. 407/396–7721; 5771 W. Irlo Bronson Memorial Hwy., tel. 407/397–2477. Entrées $8–$15. The best value is the buffet at $3.99 for breakfast, $5.99 for lunch, and $7.99 for dinner.

SLEUTH'S MYSTERY DINNER THEATER This year's pick as Orlando's top dinner show goes to Sleuth's. It's the best food and show combination in town! Your choice of Cornish hen, lasagna, or prime rib is accompanied by ample side dishes and lots of beer or wine. The show is a hilarious, interactive whodunit with audience participation that always includes kids. Ricky, my son, stole the show when he questioned a certain short suspect on his platform shoes. It's just off I-Drive. *7508 Universal Blvd., Orlando, tel. 407/363–1985. Shows nightly at varying times. $36.95 adults, $22.95 children 3–11, children under 3 free. Add $3.00 for prime rib.*

SUNDAY BRUNCH AT THE RENAISSANCE ORLANDO Kudos for Central Florida's best brunch go to the spread at this resort next to Sea World, at the southern end of I-Drive. The 150 items on the buffet vary slightly week to week but may include—as on our latest visit—succulent lamb, perfect eggs Benedict, and a lavish selection of seafood, sushi, and much more. The champagne keeps coming. *6677 Sea Harbor Dr., Orlando, tel. 407/351–5555 or 800/327–6677. $29.95 adults, $14.95 children 4–12, children under 4 free.*

CHARACTER MEALS

These events in restaurants in local hotels and theme parks put you and your kids in direct contact with your favorite characters—Mickey, Minnie, Cinderella, Woody, and the gang. These have become some of our family's most treasured memories. Figure out which characters you want to see and choose your meal based on what's available.

If the one you choose is in a theme park, you will be admitted before the park opens to the public, when it is nearly empty and the magnificent landscaping is at its most beautiful as the cast members ready the grounds for the new day. Prices vary, but are surprisingly reasonable. Plan on around $15 per adult and $8 per child 3–12 (children under 3 free).

As early as possible (up to 60 days in advance), call 407/WDW–DINE for reservations, which are usually a must. At Universal, call 407/224–6339.

Worth-It Rating ★★★★★

THEME RESTAURANTS

The first celebrity-owned theme restaurant, the **Hard Rock Café,** started out in London, but the concept really has taken root in Orlando, and, in fact, founder Robert Earl now calls Orlando home. The HRC has moved to giant new quarters in Universal's CityWalk. There, you'll also find **Bob Marley—A Tribute to Freedom,** a re-creation of the reggae star's Jamaican home, and **Jimmy Buffett's Margaritaville** (*see* Chapter 11). In Downtown Disney, Jim Belushi and Dan Aykroyd have built the **House of Blues,** Gloria Estefan brought the Latin beat with **Bongos,** and NASCAR has sanctioned the **NASCAR Café;** these join the longtime draw, **Planet Hollywood,** in the riveting blue globe on the edge of Downtown Disney (*see* Chapter 10). And at Disney's Wide World of Sports, Andre Agassi, hockey's Great Gretzky, Ken

Griffey, Jr., Joe Montana, Shaquille O'Neal, and Tiger Woods have funded the **Official All-Star Sports Cafe** (*see* Chapter 14). All of these are dazzlingly stuffed with theme memorabilia from floor to ceiling, as is my current favorite of them all:

RACE ROCK This one is from stock car king Richard Petty, Indy racer Michael Andretti, and several of their fast friends. You're served by uniformed trophy babes and pit crew under awesome race cars and boats suspended from the ceiling; you'll find loads of racing memorabilia and race-car simulators, too. But the highlight is the food, mainly mildly spicy Tex-Mex with some great barbecued ribs and chicken. In the lobby, an open-sided tractor-trailer sells all kinds of racing-logo shirts and souvenirs. *8986 International Dr., Orlando, tel. 407/248–9876. Entrées $7–$18.*
Worth-It Rating ★★★★★

CHURCH STREET STATION AND DOWNTOWN

When promoter Bob Snow came to Orlando back in the early 1970s, he wanted to revitalize its shabby downtown by turning it into a dining and shopping attraction with a historic flavor. He was wildly successful with this complex of restaurants and night spots occupying local landmarks like Orlando pioneer Stanley Bumby's hundred-year-old hardware store. For years, until Disney created Pleasure Island, Snow's Church Street Station was synonymous with Orlando nightlife in the minds of tourists. And it's still a great spot. Bob Snow and his successors scoured the world and filled the complex with 19th-century metal ceiling tiles, hand-carved woodwork, church pews, chandeliers, and stained glass. Vintage flying machines from hot-air balloons to biplanes are suspended from the ceilings, and stuffed game-animal heads adorn the walls. Rare and expensive antique vehicles are parked in the street, including a highly prized 1939 Duesenberg; a 1912 steam engine and old Pullman cars are stopped on the old train tracks. It's an eclectic visual tour de force.

Be prepared for a good time. Church Street Station is a rowdy, in-your-face place to party hearty. There are four main nightclubs, three with scheduled sets; showtimes are staggered so that you can take in a set in each during an evening. **Rosie O'Grady's** is a New Orleans-style jazz club where you can snack on a burger to the strains of an enthusiastic Dixieland band. Waiters and waitresses even dance on the bar. The **Orchid Garden Ballroom,** done up in Victorian style with rich woods and decorative glass, has a 50's-style rock band for dancing. And many major country stars have performed in the **Cheyenne Saloon and Opera House,** a Western music hall featured on numerous national TV shows. Intricate carved woodwork encloses several levels of balconies, and you can order Wild West fare—buffalo, beef steaks, chicken, and ribs (entrées $12.50 and up). **Phineas Phogg's Balloon Works,** the fourth club, is a non-stop modern dance and rock club, mostly for Gen X-ers. It's full of vintage balloonist paraphernalia. There are also a couple of restaurants.

After 6 PM, you have to pay a cover charge to enter these Church Street Station clubs, and food and beverages are extra and pricey. You're expected to buy a drink or two, at around $4 a pop, in each of its night spots. So for a couple, it's easy to go through a couple of hundred dollars in an evening. But if you don't want to spend the bucks, you can have a great time soaking up the streetmosphere and taking in the restaurants with no cover.

In turn-of-the-century-style **Lili Marlene's Aviator's Pub and Restaurant,** the prime rib comes in generous portions au jus or blackened. Entrées are about $20. The very casual **Crackers Oyster Bar,** which reminds me of the old fish camps that still dot Florida, does a more than respectable job with Florida seafood, and serves everything from raw oysters to a nice lobster-and-clam bake. The specialty is a tangy Pensacola clam chowder, but I like the chef's chili—loaded with gator meat. This place doubles as a sports bar. Entrées cost between $9.95 and $25.

Lunchtime, when Church Street Station levies no cover, is great for soaking up the atmosphere without paying. There's also an excellent Sunday brunch buffet at Lili Marlene's ($12.95). And tours of the complex are available. The area is also home to several other excellent clubs and restaurants.

Church Street Exchange, the shopping part of Church Street Station, has more than 50 specialty stores, many of them locally owned and operated. A flight-ready biplane hangs from the ceiling on the second floor, where there's also an excellent food court and **Commander Ragtime's Midway,** possibly Orlando's most extensive arcade, with about a zillion video games and claw machines. The fabulous **Buffalo Trading Company,** in the building that used to house Stanley Bumby's famous old hardware store, has all kinds of Western items including copies of an autographed picture of Butch Cassidy and the Sundance Kid and many, many fringed buckskin jackets. The **Bumby Emporium,** also huge, sells

Church Street souvenirs and lots of old-timey stuff. Out on the street, jugglers, magicians, bagpipers, and other musicians entertain day and night.

Church Street Market is just across the courtyard from Church Street Station, and if you didn't know the politics of the place, you'd think it was part of the same complex. Actually, it was cleverly created by another developer to cash in on Church Street's popularity and its advertising. Still, it has a number of worthwhile shoppertoonities. If you've never been to a **Sharper Image** store, you can visit one here. It's an attraction in itself, stocked with whatever is the state of the art in virtual reality, personal digital assistants, or electronic doodads that work underwater. **Brookstone** sells fancy hardware. And, of course, there's food: The politically incorrect **Hooter's,** a sports bar, features spicy chicken wings served by scantily clad young women. And **Jungle Jim's** has family prices and a cute jungle theme the kids will love.

The Fast Track: Church Street shows are timed so you can catch them all in an evening by going from one to the next. So that's what everybody does. Before you start out, pop your head into each of the three music spots to see which is least crowded, and start there. Then you'll be moving from venue to venue with the smallest group. *129 W. Church St., 407/422–2434 (ext. 427, to find out about tours of the complex). Cover: $17.95 adults, $11.95 children 4–12. Church Street night spots open 11 AM–2 AM, shops open 11–11.*

Worth-It Rating ★★★

SAPPHIRE SUPPER CLUB Orlando's emerging rock scene has produced such nationally famous acts as Matchbox 20, Sister Hazel, the Backstreet Boys, My Friend Steve, Von Ra, and many others. For most groups, it begins at this spot, the area's premiere showcase of new music. Several Mexican entrées and an outstanding New York steak in peppercorn sauce headline a surprisingly reasonably priced menu and a modest but nicely priced wine list. Cover charges, ticket prices, and reservation policies vary by event, but usually $5 gets you in. *54 N. Orange Ave., Downtown Orlando, tel. 407/246–1419.*

DISNEY'S BOARDWALK

My wife, Terrie, and I fell in love with this place at first sight. Designed in classic New England style to re-create the old boardwalks built along the northeastern beaches just after the turn of the century, this area has shopping, dining, lodging, and entertainment. Admission to the whole complex is free, and—here's the best part—there are no cover charges at any of the clubs! (The **BoardWalk Inn** and the **BoardWalk Villas** are both part of the Disney Vacation Club's time-share operation, but you don't have to be a time-share owner to stay there or party at the bars and clubs.) The boardwalk overlooks a lagoon facing the Yacht and Beach Club, their lighthouse, and the pirate ship at their mini-water park. Epcot is to your right, and you can see the Eiffel Tower in the distance, rising just above the BoardWalk's gazebo. Away from the water are a handful of shops and an arcade with pinball and video games (I hate arcades—Ricky hits the arcade and bang, there goes 20 bucks).

What keeps us coming back to the BoardWalk are the clubs. The **Atlantic Dance Club** recalls the ballrooms that broadcast swing music in the 1940s. The **ESPN Club** is the ultimate sports bar, with monitors everywhere—all tuned to

ESPN, of course. **Jellyroll's** is a big, rollicking night spot with two piano players at dueling grand pianos. It's the kind of place where you'd expect a cover, but there is none. In the **Belle Vue Room**, a lakeside lounge, the elegant decor and formally attired waiters make you feel like the Great Gatsby. **Big River Grill and Brewing Works** is Disney's own microbrewery; it serves British pub fare like sausages and meat pies. At **BoardWalk Bakery**, bakers make a lot of bread, along with pastries and sweets, right before your eyes. The **Flying Fish Café** serves fresh seafood. A house specialty is scallops with black truffle risotto. Reservations are accepted. Besides its highly entertaining show of pizza-twirling, **Spoodles** has a Mediterranean menu that includes some very good grilled lamb chops and a Moroccan vegetable platter. Reservations are a good idea. The bars in the BoardWalk Inn and Board-Walk Villas are every bit as atmospheric and fun. Terrie and I love all the old Atlantic City pictures displayed in these hotels—wonderful bits of nostalgia that date back to what the kids have dubbed the "gray-and-white days." There's even a picture of Atlantic City's famous diving horse.

And what would a boardwalk be without taffy? Hit **Seashore Sweets.** On our last visit, a boardwalk magician delighted the children with a show during which he was able to extract a variety of exotic objects from their ears. All in all, the BoardWalk is charming, nostalgic, and entertaining—and it offers some of the best deals on Disney property. *2101 N. Epcot Resort Blvd., Lake Buena Vista, tel. 407/939–3420; 407/WDW–DINE for restaurant reservations. Clubs open daily 7 PM–2 AM, shops open daily 9 AM–1 AM.*
Worth-It Rating ★★★★★

DINNER THEATERS

These spectacular productions, an institution in a town where everything must have a theme and entertainment value, cost literally millions of dollars to produce. Beer and wine are served.

CAPONE'S You have to know the password to get into this speakeasy featuring a Runyonesque musical comedy set in gangland Chicago in the 1930s. What the food may lack in quality, the buffet more than makes up in quantity. Costumed and in character, the servers keep the hooch coming. It's a good show and a good time. *4740 W. Irlo Bronson Memorial Hwy., Kissimmee, tel. 407/397–2378. Shows nightly at 7:30. $31.99 adults, $16.99 children 3–12, children under 3 free.* **Worth-It Rating ★★★★**

HOOP DEE DOO REVUE The long-running Wild West musical revue in WDW's Fort Wilderness features frontier guys and gals in gingham, jeans, and buckskin singing, dancing, and pratfalling their way into your heart. Small children think the slapstick's hilarious, and it's hard not to have a good time. Plus, the chicken, ribs, and country fixin's are downright good! *Fort Wilderness Campground Resort, Walt Disney World, tel. 407/WDW–DINE. Shows nightly at 5, 7:15, and 9:30. $37 adults, $19.50 children 3–11, children under 3 free.* **Worth-It Rating ★★★★**

KING HENRY'S FEAST Jesters, jugglers, acrobats, and magicians are all on hand. You might call this medieval lite–not as grand or as intense as Medieval Times (*see below*), but still a good show. The food is pretty good, too. *8984 International Dr., Orlando, tel. 407/351–5151. Shows nightly at 7*

and 9:30. $36.95 adults, $22.95 children 3–11, children under 3 free.
Worth-It Rating ★★★★

LUAU AT SEA WORLD Disney's Polynesian Luau may be the Orlando original, but this one's better and costs less. It's a full-fledged Polynesian presentation, with singers, musicians, and dancers doing the hula and the fire dance. *7007 Sea World Dr., Orlando, 407/363–2559. Shows nightly at 6:15. $35.95 adults, $25.95 children 8–12, $15.95 children 3–8, children under 3 free.*
Worth-It Rating ★★★★★

MEDIEVAL TIMES The area's most successful dinner show re-creates a joust and tournament complete with knights on horseback, sword fights, falconry, and more—accompanying a feast of chicken, barbecued ribs, soup, sangria, beer, and soda. The food is better than the competitors', the pageantry majestic, the plot romantic, the trained animals amazing, and the fights exciting and realistic. There is truly something for everyone. Though my family goes often, we always enjoy the show; it's always slightly different and seems better than the time before. It sells out early, so reserve well ahead. *4510 W. Irlo Bronson Memorial Hwy., Kissimmee, tel. 800/229–8300. Shows nightly at 8 (also at 10 in peak seasons). $38.95 adults, $23.95 children 3–12, children under 3 free.*
Worth-It Rating ★★★★★

MURDERWATCH MYSTERY DINNER THEATER You'll have to be good to figure out whodunit at this show at the Grosvenor Resort, a real killer! And the buffet is excellent. It's only on Saturday night. *1850 Hotel Plaza Blvd., Lake Buena Vista,*

407/827–6500, ext. 6103. Shows at 6 and 9, Saturday only. $33.95 adults, $17.95 children under 9, children under 3 free.
Worth-It Rating ★★★★★

OHANA Though the pay-one-price meal that goes with this Polynesian-theme show at Disney's Polynesian Village Resort is not officially all-you-can-eat, nobody has ever refused us seconds. Once I kept ordering and ordering the super-jumbo skewered-and-grilled shrimp. You get a Polynesian name and a chance to participate in the show. It's great fun and great food, both at an appealing price. *Open for breakfast 7:30 AM–11 AM and dinner 5 PM–10 PM daily. Polynesian Village Resort, Walt Disney World, tel. 407/939–3463. $20.95 adults, $14.95 children 12–16, $8.95 children 3–11, children under 3 free.*
Worth-It Rating ★★★★★

PIRATES DINNER ADVENTURE A life-size pirate ship sails seas of real water in the center of the cavernous arena that houses this huge production just off I-Drive. Circus Acrobats swing overhead as you swig beer and sangria. The chicken and ribs are not as good as the food at Medieval Times, but they're not bad, and the show is very entertaining. *6400 Carrier Dr., Orlando, tel. 800/866–AHOY, 407/248–0590. Shows Tues.–Sun. at 6:30. $37.95 adults, $22.95 children 3–11, children under 3 free.*
Worth-It Rating ★★★★

POLYNESIAN LUAU South Seas islanders perform the hula, the fire dance, and other feats of skill and artistry at this mainstay of WDW's Polynesian Village Resort. The feast features roast pork, poi, and other delicacies. One of WDW's trademark events, it still seems fresh, even after all these years. Reserve way ahead. *Polynesian Village Resort, Walt Dis-*

ney World, tel. 407/WDW–DINE. Shows daily at 4:30 and 6:45. $38 adults, $19.50 children 3–11, children under 3 free.
Worth-It Rating ★★★★

WILD BILL'S This redo of Buffalo Bill's Wild West Show has horseback riding, Native American dancing, Western dancing, sharpshooting, knife throwing, rope tossing, and just plain general hoopla! Good food, good show. *5260 W. Irlo Bronson Memorial Hwy., Kissimmee, tel. 407/351–5151. Shows nightly at 7 (sometimes also at 9:30). $36.95 adults, $22.95 children 3–11, children under 3 free.*
Worth-It Rating ★★★★

OFF THE BEATEN PATH

SAM SELTZER'S STEAK HOUSE At this landmark 20 miles north of Universal, giant plaster cows invite you to dine on prime rib from only $9.95. For $18.95 you'll get a 32-ounce cut that's the equal of any I've seen outside of Omaha. The rich, rich, rich napoleon (in a serving that's big enough for two) is my favorite of the famous homemade desserts. Definitely worth the trip. I-4 east to S.R. 436, turn right. *800 E. Altamonte Drive. (S.R. 436), Maitland, tel. 407/332–7267. Entrées $14–$26.*
Worth-It Rating ★★★★★

chapter 13

WATER PARKS

I n Central Florida you'll find more aquatic thrills than anywhere else on the planet. The Orlando area alone boasts five major water parks. There's just no reason not to get in the swim.

At each, you'll find flumes, slides, pools, tubing courses, and kiddie areas. **Flumes** are tubular, curved slides greased with a trickle of water. You race through the tube, speed through the turns, then shoot out into a shallow pool at the bottom. In some flumes, you ride on mats or in inner tubes; most are ridden bareback. In family flumes, up to six people ride together in flexible rubber tubs. **Water slides** are always open-sided and not as curvy as flumes. The key difference among the water slides is the vertical drop, the number of feet between the highest and lowest elevations. You'll also find **tube courses,** where you float on a meandering stream.

Most parks also have **wave pools**, simulating ocean action. Some have totally unique features like the reef at Typhoon Lagoon, where you swim with live sharks, and Water Mania's Wipe Out, where you can try surfing a wave.

TIPS AND BASICS Because free tubes are usually in short supply at water parks, rentals are available, along with lockers and towels. Fast food is everywhere but pricey. Picnics are allowed; glass containers and alcoholic beverages are not (nor are overly revealing bathing suits). Independent parks charge for parking; Disney water parks do not. Also remember:

- Your best value is later in the day—after 3, 4, or 5 PM, depending on park, crowd, season, and weather—when temperatures drop, early sunburns thin the crowds, and some parks offer half-price admissions.
- Never, ever leave children unsupervised. Make sure that someone is watching each child at all times. Wave pools can be chaotic.
- Don't wear anything around your neck, wrists, or ankles—it could snag and cause serious injury. If you have long hair, pull it back or keep it tied up, and keep your head up when sliding!
- Use sunblock and watch your sun time. A bad sunburn can ruin your whole vacation.
- Ladies, take note: all parks have a high-speed water slide with a giant vertical drop, 5 to 12 stories. Guys often wait at the bottom to watch women lose their tops. Gentlemen they are not.

ORLANDO AND KISSIMMEE WATER PARKS

WET 'N WILD My pick for the best-value water park, this one on I-Drive (now officially a part of Universal Studios Escape) is the original water thrill park and still offers more ride per buck than any other wetland, particularly if you follow my recommendation and purchase the Orlando FlexTicket. You'll find the thrills in the giant wave pool; on the Bomb Bay and Der Stuka, both with 76-vertical-foot-drops; in the Black Hole, a slightly terrifying flume in the dark (not for the claustrophobic); in the Bubba Tub and the Surge, two rides where your whole family can flume together; and on the Fuji Flyer, a speeding downhill raft that seats four. The Hydra-Fighter, which seats 8 to 12 lunatics, moves them around as they fire a water cannon at their fellow guests. The Lazy River, a tube-in-the-ol'-stream ride, is one of the few mellow experiences here. This high-energy park is usually crowded from late morning until late afternoon. We've always found the kiddie area inconveniently distant from the other rides. The folks at Wet 'n Wild told me that they made it this way on purpose, to keep the kids safe from high-energy traffic. They do have a point, but it's a trade-off. *Exit 30A off I–4. 6200 International Dr., near Kirkman Rd., tel. 407/351–9453. Open daily 10–5, until 11 in summer. $26.95 adults, $21.95 children 3–9, children under 3 free (½ price after 3, or after 5 in peak season).*
Worth-It Rating ★★★★★ Make that 5+ if you purchased your ticket as part of the Orlando FlexTicket.

WATER MANIA This park opposite Disney's Celebration in Kissimmee is unfortunately not keeping up with the quality of other area attractions. Still, most of the regular water-park stuff is right here: a giant wave pool, multiple flumes, several tube rides, high-vertical-drop slides, and a tubing course. The surfing attraction is one-of-a-kind: the simulated ocean waves are so realistic that actual surfing competitions have been held here. Moreover, food and rental prices are usually better than in any other park; tickets are more heavily discounted; and discounted tickets more abundant than for other water parks. *Exit 25A off I–4. 6703 W. Irlo Bronson Memorial Hwy., tel. 407/396–4994. Open daily 11–5, with earlier openings and later closings in busy seasons and warm weather. $24.95 adults, $17.95 children 3–12, children under 3 free (½ price after 3).*

Worth-It Rating ★★★ Add 1 if you get a free ticket, if you're staying on U.S. 192, of if you have small children. Subtract 1 if you pay full price.

DISNEY WATER PARKS

Disney has successfully made water parks into total themed fantasy experiences not duplicated anywhere else. If that's what you're looking for, you will probably decide that the Disney parks are worth the money. And if you're staying on Disney property and really want to do a water park, proximity and availability of Disney transportation make one of these attractions an obvious choice. For ticket prices, *see* Chapter 2.

TYPHOON LAGOON The landmark of this attraction near Walt Disney World Village is a ship that was tossed atop a mountain during a terrible storm (or so the story goes). Forget

the fact that there aren't any hills here in Florida—this is Disney, where anything is possible. Highlights include the world's largest wave pool, a pair of incredible vertical slides, three white-water raft rides, and a river ride, which takes you easily from place to place and to the well-equipped tykes' area called Ketchakiddie Creek. The unduplicated specialty of the house is a tropical snorkeling adventure where you actually swim with small live sharks (safely; I've done it, and I'm not brave. The hardest part for me was the icy water). *Exit 26B off I–4, tel. 407/560–4141. Open daily 10–5 (until 7 or later in summer).*
Worth-It Rating ★★★★ Add 1 if you're doing it on a Disney pass.

BLIZZARD BEACH Did I say Typhoon Lagoon's theme is far-fetched? Disney has abandoned all pretense of plausibility in this park. Here's the story: the weather turned freakish; a snowstorm blanketed Florida; Disney tried to cash in by building a ski resort; the sun returned; and Blizzard Beach was born.

Mount Gushmore, at its center, is the source of multiple flumes. The high-vertical-drop slide is the world's tallest at 120 feet (12 stories). A radar unit clocks your descent on a big digital display at speeds of up to 60 mph. The chairlift is a nice touch. So is Tike's Peak, a conveniently located, kid-size version of almost all the rest of the water park. At the Blizzard Beach Ski Patrol Training Camp, you can try to jump across floating simulated ice floes without falling in. The result looks sort of like *Baywatch* on ice. *Exit 26B off I–4, west of World Dr. on Osceola Pkwy., opposite the Disney All-Star Resorts, tel. 407/560–3400. Open daily 10–5 (until 7 or later in summer).*
Worth-It Rating ★★★★★ Make that 5+ if you're doing it on a Disney pass.

RIVER COUNTRY From the beginning, Disney has billed this park as a "re-creation of the ol' swimmin' hole." It's a good one. While no longer Disney's premier water park or even a state-of-the-art water attraction by today's standards, it holds up well for what it is, a rip-roarin' chance to feel like Huck Finn on the mighty Mississippi! And admission here is cheaper than at other Disney water parks.

Spreading out from its own sandy beach on the shore of a natural Florida lake, River Country has old-time rope swings, flumes, raft rides, and a smallish kiddie section (not particularly convenient). There are nature trails and a playground, and, for those who may not like the feel and aroma of Florida lake water, an oversize heated and chlorinated swimming pool.

Water launches to River Country leave regularly from both the Magic Kingdom and Disney's Contemporary Resort. *Exit 26A off I-4 (follow signs to Fort Wilderness), off Fort Wilderness Tr., tel. 407/824-2760. Open daily 10-5 (until 7 or later in summer).*

Worth-It Rating ★★★ Add 1 if you're a Mark Twain fan. Subtract 1 if you like your water chlorinated.

chapter 14

THE WIDER WORLD OF SPORTS

Orlando visitors often remark that everything here seems to be its own "World." In addition to Walt Disney World and Sea World, there's Bargain World, Boat World, even Flea World—a flea market, not a dog kennel. Now that Disney owns ABC and its sister network ESPN, it has entered the wide world of sports in a very big way. Add the golf and other sports activities, and Orlando may soon be Sports World.

DISNEY'S WIDE WORLD OF SPORTS

"If you build it, they will come," we learned in the fantasy baseball movie *Field of Dreams*. Disney is betting heavily that there are enough sports nuts—tourists and locals—to support an Orlando field of dreams on 200 acres at the southwest corner of its property, near Blizzard Beach. The sprawling yellow complex, designed to house events televised on Disney's own ESPN, conjures up images of the mostly vanished baseball parks that helped to define the sport in the first half of this century. But there's much more than baseball here.

Here, you can visit a Basketball Hall of Fame, watch the Atlanta Braves in spring training or Harlem Globetrotters exhibitions, or take in Amateur Athletic Union national track-and-field events. You'll also find opportunities to learn, practice, and refine your own skills in almost any sport imaginable.

SPECTATOR SPORTS FACILITIES The largest structure in the complex is the **Fieldhouse.** Inside are six basketball courts and facilities for martial arts, table tennis, weight lifting, wrestling, boxing, fencing, gymnastics, handball, and even badminton. Baseball is also a big deal. The **Ballpark** is particularly charming and old-timey. The Atlanta Braves have spring training here, and farm teams are scheduled to play here at other times. The Ballpark is part of the **Baseball Quadraplex,** which includes three additional ball fields of major-league dimensions, one fully lighted. The Ballpark can seat nearly 10,000; these accommodate just a few hundred. And watch out, Williamsport. With their permanent bleachers, scoreboards, and dugouts, these two **Youth Baseball Fields** were designed for major events like the Little League World Series, which currently takes place in that central Pennsylvania town. Softball anyone? The four regulation softball fields in the **Softball Quadraplex** are lighted for night play. In addition, there are four white-sand-beach **volleyball courts,** a spiffy **track-and-field complex,** four **soccer fields** with international specifications, and a **tennis complex** with 11 fast-dry courts (the United States Tennis Association's Men's Clay Court Championships are slated to take place here annually in spring). This is all in addition to the **Velodrome** built for the Centennial Olympics in Atlanta, which the Imagineers had disassembled, shipped to Orlando, and reassembled, steel girder by steel girder, on this site. Call Disney's Sports Line as you firm up your travel dates to see what's on (tel. 407/363–6600), and schedule accordingly. And do this as far ahead as you can, since Disney events regularly sell out. Also look into sports-vacation and event-related packages, available through Walt Disney Travel Company Sports Reservations (tel. 407/939–7810).

THE NFL EXPERIENCE On a regulation football field here at Wide World of Sports, National Football League–trained pros supervise visitors who want to try their hand at any of 10 different events like passing, kicking, running, and all the other stuff football players do.

OFFICIAL ALL-STAR SPORTS CAFÉ This sports bar with a difference comes to you courtesy of tennis star Andre Agassi, hockey's Great Gretzky, Ken Griffey, Jr., Joe Montana, the Orlando Magic's former star Shaquille O'Neal, current local resident Tiger Woods, and Orlando's own Robert Earl, who founded both the Hard Rock Café and Planet Hollywood. Watch any of the numerous screens for live events along with taped highlights from every major sport as you chow down on all-American steak and seafood.

GOLF

Along with its many other distinctions, Central Florida is the number-one golf destination in the world, with more holes of golf than almost any other part of the United States. I'm not a golfer but for those of you who are, here's my take on what's out there.

DISNEY'S 99 HOLES The passionate golfers all know that Walt Disney World, taken as a whole, is one of the largest and best golf resorts anywhere, with its six very good courses with very good facilities. These are in three locations on-property—near the Magic Kingdom, at the Armed Forces R&R station known as Shades of Green; near Downtown Disney; and near Fort Wilderness. Each area has complete facilities, everything from a PGA-staffed instructional program to a pro shop, locker room, snack bar, and restaurant.

In theory, all courses are open to the public. However, guests at resorts on Disney property and those with hotel reservations can make reservations up to 60 days in advance with a major credit card (tel. 407/WDW–GOLF or 407/939–4653), and Disney's own guests may have an edge in getting a tee time when the getting is tough.

Near the Magic Kingdom: The **Palm**, designed by Joe Lee, is the toughest Disney course, cut through the dense pine forest. The **Magnolia**, another Joe Lee test, is the longest course at WDW. Extra-long fairways challenge the most powerful drivers, along with 11 water hazards and 97 sand bunkers; the one on the sixth looks remarkably like the well-known silhouette of a certain mouse. Right next door is **Oak Trail**, a nine-hole, par-36 walking course with relatively short fairways and fast greens. The smallest of Disney's courses, it makes a perfect little golf outing on a tight family vacation schedule.

Near Fort Wilderness: **Eagle Pines** was created by Pete Dye, with a low profile and roughs of pine needles and sand. **Osprey Ridge,** designed by Tom Fazio, is links-style, with elevated greens and tees, nine water holes, and over 70 bunkers scattered through pine forests, palmetto scrub, and marshy stands of Florida cypress.

Near Downtown Disney: **Lake Buena Vista,** another Joe Lee design, is the oldest of the Disney courses, with an island green on the seventh hole.

HEADS UP, DUFFERS! The average player can't go far wrong on almost any of the dozens of area courses, many fairly inexpensive. Several are worth a detour, though. **Arnold Palmer's Bay Hill Club and Lodge** (9000 Bay Hill Blvd., Orlando, tel. 407/876–2429), near Universal Studios Escape, is the home of Arnold Palmer's home course, and as you would expect, is consistently top-ranked by *Golf Digest* magazine. Nearby, in the shadow of the area's tallest and most beautiful hotel, **Mariott's Orlando World Center** (1 World Center Dr., Orlando 32821, tel. 407/239–4200), are 18 more holes of perfectly manicured golf. The hotel is also the home of Nick Faldo's Golf School. The 45-hole Jack Nicklaus layout at the **Hyatt Regency Grand Cypress Resort** (1 N. Jacaranda, Orlando, tel. 407/239–1234), directly behind Downtown Disney, is a faithful re-creation of historic Scottish courses; PGA-certified pros at its golf academy video your strokes.

chapter 15

GRAND OLD FLORIDA ATTRACTIONS AND OTHER DIVERSIONS

Entrepreneurs from all over the world flock to Orlando in the belief that where there are millions of tourists, there are millions of dollars to go around. One company spent a small fortune on a theme park that would have featured a levitating hotel designed to hover four feet above the ground, supported only by psychic energy. (I'm not kidding.) Such places come and go pretty quickly. Some attractions are real survivors—vintage Florida landmarks that predate Walt Disney World, and even Disneyland, by decades. These are good enough to merit a mention, perhaps even a visit. I cover the best of them all in this chapter, along with WDW destinations—like Disney Institute and Discovery Island—that are real alternatives to a day in the parks.

Should you bother at all? Obviously some of what you'll find is unique to the area. As for the rest, I'd advise you to think twice before you spend your time on the kinds of attractions you'll find at home: In Central Florida, with its huge pool of visitors, they'll probably be bigger, better, newer, and nicer—but they won't necessarily be a good deal. If you read my Chapter 1 and took the time to calculate the hourly cost of your vacation—or even if you just use my hypothetical $37 per hour—you know that it's costing you at least $30 to $40 per waking hour just to be here. When you add that figure to the cost of, say, go-cart rides at $3 or more a lap, you are easily spending $50 to $60 an hour on go-carting.

Or look at it this way. If you can expect to see about one ride or show every 45 minutes in a theme park, a reasonable estimate, you can do about 16 rides during a 12-hour day. If a theme-park ticket costs you around $40, the cost works out to $2.50 a ride. Some of the smaller attractions I describe below, like Paintball World, are full-day experiences that you may well want to choose instead of one of the theme parks. Most, however, will set you back about $10 each, or 4 times as much as a single theme-park ride. To duplicate a theme-park day with its 16 adventures, you would be spending an average of $160 per person per day.

Obviously, you don't want to do that. However, you might be mixing some time by the pool with shopping and a couple of other fun things, and that's where these attractions come in. So, if your family includes a real go-cart fan or miniature-golf fanatic, or if you have an hour or so to kill on an afternoon, don't let me stop you. I'm just here to help you decide what's worth it and what's not. As an attractions connoisseur, I can tell you that, within categories, the biggest difference is location. Don't waste gas driving to Kissimmee if you're staying on International Drive.

Here are my top picks, with my favorites listed first in each category.

GRAND OLD FLORIDA ATTRACTIONS

SILVER SPRINGS In 1996, while we were all congratulating Disney on bringing the theme park to Central Florida 25 years before, Silver Springs quietly celebrated its 100th birthday. Although it takes an hour and a half to get here, my family visits this 350-acre park at least once a year. It's built around crystal-clear Mammoth Spring, the world's largest natural artesian spring formation and the source of Florida's awesome Silver River. Glass-bottom boat tours give you a perfect view of dugout canoes on the river bottom, where they sank before the arrival of Columbus. There are also concerts by big-name entertainers, a narrated cruise down the unspoiled tropical river, and a Jeep trip through a dense cypress and live-oak forest, where you'll see sloth, exotic deer, and antelope. And, usually in June, July, and August, the springs are opened for swimming. The drive here is through Florida's magnificent horse country, as significant to Thoroughbred racing as Kentucky's bluegrass. The park is just off I–75, a mile east of Ocala on Route 40. The all-in-one ticket is a great value. Tip: Bring insect repellent—would you believe that in an attraction with insects the size of house cats, there is none to be found in the entire park? *5656 E. Silver Springs Blvd., Silver Springs, tel. 352/236–2121 or 800/234–7458. $29.95 plus tax adults, $20.95 plus tax children 3–9, children under 3 free. Open daily 9–5:30, longer during school vacations.* **Worth-It Rating ★★★★**

GATORLAND Back in 1949, when Owen Godwin founded the self-proclaimed Alligator Capital of the World, Florida had dozens of alligator parks. But only Godwin had the foresight to put his just a few miles from the piece of land that later caught the eye of a Californian named Walt Disney. Today, alligators are so thick they are literally on top of each other. There are three shows here: **Gator Jumparoo** pits a hungry gator against a chicken in a leap for lunch—that is, a trainer holds a raw chicken above the water and a hungry gator leaps to retrieve it. (This show is best first thing in the morning, when the gators haven't eaten since supper.) **Gator Wrestlin'**, an old Florida tradition, pits a full-size man against a man-size gator in an honest-to-goodness wrestling match. The goal of the man is to end up on top, while keeping the gator's powerful mouth clamped shut. The goal of the gator is not clear. And in **Snakes of Florida,** you'll see deadly Florida rattlesnakes, water moccasins, and coral snakes in cages and in demonstrations. You can also ride an old-time narrow-gauge choo-choo through some genuine Florida swampland in undeveloped park areas or go for a walk in the same terrain. (But beware: the swamp wildlife is real and some of those reptiles have no respect.) Back in the center of the park at **Pearl's Smokehouse,** you can actually see a man eating gator—women and children can eat some, too. Fried gator nuggets taste a lot like chicken. (Wouldn't you have guessed?) Gatorland is also one of the world's largest commercial alligator farms. The thousands of gators on the grounds are not just there for your entertainment. They are also destined to serve humankind as shoes, belts, luggage, and meat. So if you're shopping for gator goods, the gift shop here is the place. Be prepared to hold your nose. Like all wildlife parks, this can be stinky, especially in the

hot sun. *14501 S. Orange Blossom Trail (U.S. 441), between Orlando·and Kissimmee, tel. 407/855–5496 or 800/393–5297. $16.93 adults, $7.48 children 3–12, children under 3 free. Open daily 9–6.*
Worth-It Rating ★★★★

HOMOSASSA SPRINGS STATE WILDLIFE PARK The main attraction at this 174-acre state park is an underwater viewing area in a natural spring that is home to Florida's famous endangered sea cow, the manatee. There are also ranger tours and nature trails. It's three hours from Orlando via U.S. 19. *9225 W. Fish Bowl Dr., Homosassa Springs, tel. 352/628–2311. $7.95 adults, $4.95 children 3–12, children under 3 free. Open daily 9–5:30.*
Worth-It Rating ★★★★ Add half a star if you're in the area.

WEEKI WACHEE SPRINGS CITY OF MERMAIDS I have to admit that back in the 1960s, when I first saw the ads for an underwater show featuring "live mermaids," I thought the idea was bizarre. It is. But it's still entertaining to see these "live mermaids"—young women performing a gracefully choreographed submarine spectacle, complete with narration and music. (They pause frequently to sip air from bubbling hoses around the set.) The current production is of Hans Christian Andersen's "The Little Mermaid," a story also used by another theme park whose name escapes me just now. Other attractions at this park 45 minutes north of Tampa include a wilderness river cruise, exotic bird shows, and a petting zoo. Adjacent **Buccaneer Bay** is the state's only water park at a natural spring. *6131 Commercial Way (U.S. 19 and Rte. 50), Weeki Wachee, tel. 352/596–2062*

GRAND OLD FLORIDA ATTRACTIONS

or 800/678–9335. $16.95 adults, $12.95 children ages 3–10, children under 3 free. Open daily 10–5, longer during school vacations.
Worth-It Rating ★★★ +

BOK TOWER GARDENS Speaking of bizarre, who knows what moved an eccentric 1920s millionaire, *Ladies Home Journal* founder Edward Bok, to create one of the world's premier carillon towers in the middle of nowhere. Now a National Historic Landmark, 279-foot Bok Tower has recitals daily at 3 PM, and the bells ring every half hour beginning at 10. The adjoining botanical garden contains 36 species of indigenous plants that are rare or endangered. The complex is 3 miles north of Lake Wales. *Burns Ave. and Tower Blvd. (on U.S. 27 and Route 60), Lake Wales, tel. 941/676–1408. $4 adults, $1 children 5–12, children under 5 free. Open daily 8–6.*
Worth-It Rating ★★★ Add 1 if you're in the neighborhood anyway.

CYPRESS GARDENS Nowadays, theme-park water-ski shows are almost as common as parades. But the first were staged by Dick Pope, Sr., at the 200-acre garden complex he established in 1936, and they are still world-class. Sparkling lakes and ancient cypress swamps surround the park, which is home to 8,000 varieties of plants and flowers from 90 different countries. You can tour the gardens on your own, with a guide, or on a scenic boat ride. Other attractions include circus acts, an ice-skating revue, reptile and birds-of-prey shows, Floridiana, shops and restaurants, children's rides, and the spectacular Butterfly Conservatory, with thousands of species. Don't miss the Southern Belles, the park's famed hostesses, who wear showy antebellum dresses. *Off U.S. 27, about 22 mi south of I–4, near Winter Haven, between*

Orlando and Tampa, tel. 941/324–2111, 800/237–4826, or 800/282–2123 in Florida. $30.95 adults, $20.95 ages 6–17, children under 6 free. Open daily 9:30–9.
Worth-It Rating ★★★★

INSIDE WALT DISNEY WORLD

DISNEY INSTITUTE A pet project of Disney CEO Michael Eisner, this is Disney's answer to Chautauqua, western New York State's venerable learning retreat. In a lush, wooded setting on WDW property, near Downtown Disney, the Disney Institute offers 60 programs in eight areas of interest, ranging from film and the performing arts to cooking, gardening, and sports. Programs are conducted by highly qualified instructors and visiting celebrities. There are evening programs and performances (ballet, films, comedy, and beyond) in an outdoor amphitheater, a small movie house, and an even smaller theater. Fees start at about $89 per person for a single day for adults and children over 7, including 2 learning sessions, use of the fitness facility, and admission to that evening's performance. A complete program for kids aged 10 to 17 and a day camp for kids from 7 to 9 make the Institute family-friendly. *Tel. 407/827–4800.*
Worth-It Rating ★★★★★

FANTASIA GARDENS MINIATURE GOLF The biggest and best miniature golf course I've ever seen is a must-see for miniature golf enthusiasts. Enchanted broomsticks, dancing elephants, and other characters from *Fantasia* are the obstacles; musical fanfares from the film reward successful putts. If you have time to play only one miniature golf course in Orlando,

it should be this one, which is next to the Swan and Dolphin hotels, near Epcot. *Epcot Resorts Blvd., tel. 407/560–8760. $9 adults, $7 children ages 3–9. Open daily 10 AM–11 pm.*
Worth-It Rating ★★★★

DISCOVERY ISLAND Walt Disney had a special place in his heart for this attraction on an 11-acre island across Bay Lake and the Seven Seas Lagoon from the Magic Kingdom. It is said that when he picked the original parcel of land that was to become Walt Disney World, he earmarked the island as a wildlife sanctuary.

The result is now a zoological park accredited by the American Association of Zoological Parks and Aquariums, home to 250 plant species, not to mention over 100 species of animals, many threatened with extinction. Discovery Island is also the site of one of the world's largest walk-through aviaries, and there are small shows, including "Animal Encounters," "Feathered Friends" (with parrots), the "Birds of Prey" show, and "Reptile Relations." Times vary; shows may be canceled if it rains or storms.

You can get there via WDW transportation from the Magic Kingdom, the Contemporary Resort, and Fort Wilderness; if you're driving, use the Fort Wilderness exit off I–4 and follow signs to Fort Wilderness, where you can catch a launch to the island. Special nature programs are available; call 407/824–3784 for information. *See* Chapter 2 for fees.
Worth-It Rating ★★★ Add 2 if you love nature.

ELECTRICAL WATER PAGEANT On view several times a night all year long, this is like a floating version of the Magic Kingdom's nightly Main Street Electrical Parade. You can watch it from the beach at the Polynesian Village Resort, where it starts nightly at about 9 PM. Then it moves to the Contemporary, the Grand Floridian, and Fort Wilderness. You can also see some of it from the Magic Kingdom's turnstiles area near the ferry and monorail. Ask at Guest Relations in City Hall for times. There's no charge.

Worth-It Rating ★★★★★ How can you not love something that's dazzling, this entertaining—and free!

INTERNATIONAL DRIVE AND ORLANDO

ORLANDO SCIENCE CENTER AND LOCH HAVEN PARK As you would expect in the city with neighbors like the Walt Disney Company, Lockheed-Martin, and NASA, Orlando's hands-on children's museum is terrific. It's enormous, with a planetarium and observatory at the top, towering over Orlando's lovely old Loch Haven Park. Exhibits change monthly but are always professionally mounted, with lots of high-tech razzle-dazzle. The planetarium regularly presents laser light shows.

Loch Haven Park is also home to the city's art museum, which exhibits many kinds of art from primitive to contemporary. The **Orlando Historical Museum** is the local archive; most artifacts are from the early part of this century. The **Central Florida Civic Theater** and **Children's Theater** are also here; shows change monthly. Loch Haven Park itself is a lovely, shady, lakeside preserve where you'll find kite fly-ins, balloon meets, and model-boat club meetings. This is the real Orlando, with an exotic mix of the Old South and big money. *Science Center: 810 E. Rollins St., Orlando, tel. 407/896–7151. $9.50 adults, $6.75 children 3–11,*

*children under 3 free. Open Mon.–Thurs. 9–5, Sat. and Fri.
9–9, Sun. noon–5; laser shows Fri. and Sat. 9, 10, 11, and
midnight.*
Worth-It Rating ★★★★★

RIPLEY'S BELIEVE IT OR NOT! One of the best photo-ops in
town, this must-see building was intentionally designed to
look like it's falling over into one of Florida's many sinkholes.
Inside is a collection of oddities gathered by explorer/writer/
cartoonist Robert Ripley and his successors, including two-
headed animals. When my Ricky was six, he got so spooked
that he ran out of the place. *8201 International Dr., near Sand
Lake Rd., tel. 800/998–4418. $10.95 adults, $7.95 children 4–12,
children under 4 free. Open daily 9 AM–midnight.*
Worth-It Rating ★★★★★

MOVIE RIDER Bigger than *Star Tours,* but only about half the
size of *Back to the Future,* this simulator ride's main appeal is
the length of the experience—about a half hour in the ca-
reening chair. Trivia: This attraction is from Iwerks Entertainment, the company founded by Ub Iwerks—Walt Disney's
original partner. *8815 International Dr., tel. 407/352–0050, and
5390 W. Irlo Bronson Memorial Hwy., Kissimmee, tel. 407/396–
4185. $8.95 adults, $6.95 children under 10. Open weekdays 11–
11, weekends 10 AM–midnight.*
Worth-It Rating ★★★★

AIR ORLANDO Helicopter rides and a view of scenic Orlando, for a price. *8990 International Dr., tel. 407/352–1753.
$20–$395 adults, $20–$225 children 2–12, children under 2 free.
Open Mon.–Sun. 11-9.*
Worth-It Rating ★★★

CONGO RIVER GOLF & EXPLORATION CO. A giant water-fall, artificial mountains, and jungle props simulate high adventure at this mini golf course near Wet 'n Wild. The humongous waterfalls cool you off, even on hot days. There are tunnels, ramps, and rocks, and plaques tell stories at each hole. This one has a twin in Kissimmee. But, as I said, Fantasia's tops. *6312 International Dr., tel. 407/352–0042. $7.50–$10.95, children under 4 free. Open daily 10 AM–11 PM.*
Worth-It Rating ★★★

PIRATE'S COVE ADVENTURE GOLF At these pirate-theme miniature golf layouts, the giant waterfalls are inexplicably full of blue food coloring. This is our next-favorite miniature golf course after Fantasia. *8601 International Dr., Orlando, tel. 407/352–7378; Crossroads Center, I–4 Exit 27, Lake Buena Vista, tel. 407/827–1242. $6.50–$10 adults, $5.50–$9 children 4–12, children under 4 free. Open daily 9–11:30.*
Worth-It Rating ★★★

TERROR ON CHURCH STREET This big haunted house in downtown Orlando near Church Street Station is full of things that go bump in the night. Most of it is in the dark, with black light for effects. It may be too intense for little kids. *135 S. Orange Ave., tel. 407/649–3327. $13 adults, $11 children 3–17, children under 3 free. Open daily 7 PM–midnight.*
Worth-It Rating ★★★ Add 2 if you're visiting with teens.

AROUND KISSIMMEE

MEDIEVAL LIFE Actors portray typical villagers in this re-creation of a medieval town, demonstrating falconry and crafts such as carving and weaving. Check out the dungeon and torture chamber. It's free when you attend Medieval Times, the area's big dinner show. *4510 W. Irlo Bronson Memorial Hwy., Kissimmee, tel. 800/229–8300. $8 adults, $6 children 3–12, children under 3 free. Open daily 4:30–8.*
Worth-It Rating ★★★★★ That's if you see it before or after attending Medieval Times. Otherwise, subtract 2.

PAINTBALL WORLD If your vacation isn't complete without a paintball war in the Florida sun, don't miss this unique experience off U.S. 192 at its eastern end, behind Old Town. In the paintball world, this is the most famous playing field, appearing on ESPN's Annual International Paintball World Championships. In the games here, platoons of make-believe soldiers armed with real guns shoot at each other with exploding balls of red paint. Many families come to work out their aggressions. You can shoot your spouse here, legally! This is a grown-up version of Capture the Flag—definitely not kid stuff (and in fact, children under 10 are not allowed to play). There's a spectator area for noncombatants. *2701 Holiday Trail, tel. 407/396–4199. Pump gun $18.95, semiautomatic $25 for the day. 20-min games with 10-min breaks weekends 10–4 and on some weekdays in peak seasons; closed most weekdays.*
Worth-It Rating ★★★★★

GREEN MEADOWS FARM This warm-and-fuzzy attraction, 5 miles off U.S. 192, combines a petting zoo and a tour of a working farm with hayrides, cow-milking, and more. *1368 S. Poinciana Blvd., tel. 407/846–0770. $13, children under 3 free. Open daily 9:30–5; last tour at 4.*

Worth-It Rating ★★★★ Add 1 if you're bringing little city kids who've never had another chance to see a farm.

OLD TOWN This has always been a family favorite, with rides and shopping on a re-created brick main street. The shopping is mostly for nostalgia collectors—one nifty store specializes in things for Jimmy Buffett fans. The kart track and arcade are excellent. And the Old Town Photo Gallery, where you dress up to have antique-style photos taken, is one of the largest such operations in the U.S. *5770 W. Irlo Bronson Memorial Hwy., Kissimmee, tel. 407/396–4888. General admission free; price for individual attractions varies. Open daily 10 AM–11 PM; rides operate 12 AM–11 PM.*

Worth-It Rating ★★★★

CONGO RIVER GOLF & EXPLORATION CO. This spot, 3 miles east of I-4, is a twin of the Congo River Golf on I-Drive (*see above*). *4777 W. Irlo Bronson Memorial Hwy., tel. 407/396–6900. $7.50–$11.50, children under 4 free. Open Sun.–Thurs. 10 AM–11 PM, Fri.–Sat. 10 AM–midnight.*

Worth-It Rating ★★★

JUNGLELAND This animal park, which recently made national news when a lion escaped, is neither as big as Gatorland nor as funky as Titusville's Jungle Adventure, but they're working hard to upgrade it. If you want to see some gators without committing to a day at Gatorland, this is a good bet. *4580 W. Irlo Bronson Memorial Hwy., Kissimmee, tel. 407/396–*

1012. $11.95 adults, $6.95 children 3–11, children under 3 free. Open daily 9–6.
Worth-It Rating ★★★

PIRATE'S ISLAND ADVENTURE GOLF More pirate golf (*see* Pirate's Cove, *above*). *4330 W. Irlo Bronson Memorial Hwy., Kissimmee, tel. 407/396–4660. $5.50 adults, $4 children 4–12, children under 4 free. Open daily 9 AM–11:30 PM.*
Worth-It Rating ★★★

chapter 16

THE SPACE COAST

The fastest route is the Beeline Expressway, Route 528. For a more scenic alternative, take I–4 east then the East–West Expressway to Route 50. This safe and modern four-lane state highway was the original route between Orlando and the coast and passes several authentic Florida attractions that I recommend.

I'm a space kid. My father's transfer with the missile program is what brought my family to Florida from Maryland in the 1950s. I'm constantly amazed by the enormous discrepancy between the number of people who plan to visit the Kennedy Space Center and the number who actually make it there. I have always attributed this phenomenon to the ever-increasing length of stays covered by the Disney passes and to Disney's apparent effort to take an ever-larger percentage of every Florida vacationer's dollar. It's a shame that so many people travel so far and get so close to the space center only to miss it—one of the truly outstanding experiences in Central Florida.

Created at the height of the Cold War, the space center is surrounded by a large buffer area, a tropical wilderness that is one of the last places where you can see the Sunshine State the way it used to be. On the way in or out, we often stop to watch alligators sun themselves on the banks of roadside streams. (Please don't get out to feed them—tourists are among their favorite foods.)

My ideal Florida vacation includes the Space Center, some of the grand old Florida attractions described in Chapter 15, and the East Coast beaches described in Chapter 17. I advise you to spend a few days seeing theme parks, and then drop in on the real Florida. If you leave early enough, you'll see the rose-colored dawn and a sunrise over the primeval wilderness just east of metropolitan Orlando. Plan an extra day and you can travel back in time to an original Florida settlement, take an airboat ride across the saw grass, and see an authentic old reptile park, all within 50 miles of Orlando.

WHAT TO SEE

JOHN F. KENNEDY SPACE CENTER VISITOR CENTER I get goose bumps here. The impact of visiting the site of the greatest scientific achievements in the history of humanity simply cannot be overstated. Brave Americans first breached the stratosphere and shot to the moon from here, and they still journey into space on a regular basis. It astonishes me that just an hour from my suburban neighborhood, I can see and touch the actual artifacts that transported all of us to the edge of reality.

Located in the U.S. Government NASA complex, this attraction is also Central Florida's best visitor value. You enter the grounds for free, park for free, and walk around for free.

The visitor center is also free. Here, exhibits showcase everything that's been in space, from pressure suits to capsules that carried astronauts aloft. Don't miss the lunar landing module and the film shot on the moon—not just the video that we've all seen a zillion times, but 16mm movies filmed and narrated by astronauts on the moon. At the **Launch Status Center,** you'll receive up-to-the-minute briefings on missions in progress and get a behind-the-scenes look at what's going on at Kennedy Space Center. Outside, you can walk through the space shuttle *Explorer,* a complete, full-size spacecraft; photograph spacecraft in the Rocket Garden; and have your picture taken with Spaceman, the Space Center's own character, who wears a lunar-landing pressure suit. Forget your camera? Show some ID and borrow one for free.

There is a separate charge for the films shown in two of the world's largest IMAX theaters, with screens 50 feet high (about five stories). Some of the footage in these launch documentaries, shown nowhere else on earth, was shot in space by astronauts using an ultra-high-resolution camera; some was taken from the Hubble telescope. *Mission to Mir,* narrated by astronauts Norm Thagard, John Blaha, and Shannon Lucid, contains live-action shots of Mir, the now-infamous Russian space station. *The Dream Is Alive* is an overview of the space program narrated by Walter Cronkite. *L5: First City in Space* is the center's first 3D IMAX film. Using data from NASA and leading scientists, the production combines live action with 3D animation to take you on a tour of a space city, through the Candor Chasm of Mars, and finally to the surface of a comet. Unless you're in training to be an astronaut, this is the closest you'll come to being in space.

You can also sign up for two guided bus tours to the launch pads for the Mercury, Gemini, and Apollo capsules, as well as those of the current shuttle program. (There is a charge for these tours.) The more popular **Kennedy Space Center Tour** visits the Apollo launch area, the shuttle launch area, and most of the current operational sites. You'll see a Saturn rocket like the ones that propelled the Apollo flights—the largest rocket ever built—displayed horizontally in a pavilion where you can view every inch of it; and lots of real moon memorabilia, including a lunar rock. The **Cape Canaveral Tour** visits the old Mercury and Gemini pads with a stop at the Air Force Museum. (Note that tour itineraries change from time to time, and this tour is not always available, particularly in slow seasons.)

What amazes me about the early space program is how low-tech it was. By current standards, we sent those people up in tin cans propelled by firecrackers. Close inspection of the rocket engines reveals pipes and fittings that would be at home on a plumber's truck and gizmos that are no more sophisticated than my lawn mower. Many of today's luxury cars have more powerful onboard computers and navigation systems than the one Apollo used to go to the moon. One space capsule you can actually poke your head inside left the earth and returned controlled by nothing but row upon row of on-and-off toggle switches. I could spend literally hours standing and staring, trying to imagine the courage that our astronauts must have possessed to hurtle into the void at incredible speeds in those tiny flying buckets.

The Fast Track: Buy your movie and tour tickets first, then proceed through the Visitor Center and the other attractions accordingly. Lines usually move pretty well. Except on launch days.

On launch days in peak season, roads may be so clogged that you can't even get near the place. The park may be closed without notice, and an admission charge is levied and special tickets required (which you must purchase in advance from the address below and pick up on the day before the launch in person, with photo ID). It's a lot of trouble, and there's a chance the launch could still be scrubbed. Even so, I urge you to go if the opportunity presents itself. As jaded as I am from living in the world's playground, I know of no more unforgettable experience.

Bites: In the food court, you chow down on Italian food, southern fare like fried catfish, and cold sandwiches. **Mila's,** a sit-down restaurant with old jukebox and art-deco motifs, reminds me of Florida the way it was when I first came here. The food is like the food our moms used to fix: shepherd's pie, Salisbury steak, ham with pineapple, Yankee pot roast, and chicken pot pie. This place is neat!

Rte. 405, East Titusville, tel. 800/KSC–INFO in Florida, 407/452–2121. Open daily 9–6:30, usually longer in peak seasons. Admission free; launch days $10, children under 3 free (purchase tickets in advance with a credit card at 407/452–2121, extension 4343). Bus tours: $14 adults, $10 children 3–11, children under 3 free. 3D IMAX movie: $7 adults, $5 children 3–11, children under 3 free. Crew Pass (bus tour and 3D IMAX film): $19 adults, $15 children 3–11, children under 3 free. Other IMAX movies: $7.50 adults, $5.50 children 3–11, children under 3 free. **Worth-It Rating ★★★★★**

U.S. ASTRONAUT HALL OF FAME One small step from the gates of the Space Center is this attraction created by the Mercury Seven Foundation, the original Mercury astronauts and their families. The astronauts have contributed mementos, films, photos, and artifacts to make this a worthwhile extension of the Space Center experience. Shuttle simulators provide realistic facsimiles of astronaut experiences. This is also the home of the **U.S. Space Camp,** a summer camp that gives children and adults the chance to train for space travel on equipment used by early astronauts. It's the right stuff! *6225 Vectorspace Blvd., Titusville, tel. 407/269–6100 (Hall of*

Fame) or 407/267–3184 (Space Camp). $13.95 adults, $9.95 children 3–12, children under 3 free. Open daily 9–5.
Worth-It Rating ★★★★★

ON THE WAY

FORT CHRISTMAS COUNTY PARK This absolutely free attraction, just off Route 50, is a genuine 19th-century Florida settlement that grew up around a wooden fort built during the Seminole wars. The fort's name, derived from its dedication on Christmas Day, makes the town's post office one of the busiest in the United States. Around Christmas, don't miss the historical reenactment of the battle of Fort Christmas. *23760 E. Colonial Dr., Christmas, tel. 407/568–5053. Free. Open daily dawn–dusk.*
Worth-It Rating ★★★★★ Subtract 2 or 3 if you aren't nearby.

JUNGLE ADVENTURES Roadside wildlife parks like this very reasonably priced spot were once Florida's main attractions. Most have closed. Some, like Gatorland, have grown modern and slick. Jungle Adventure is Cracker-style, recalling the old backwoods types that used to roam, hunt, and homestead Florida's swamps and forests. It contains about a zillion alligators, a petting zoo, and a small refuge for endangered species, including eagles and panthers. *26205 E. Route 50, Christmas, tel. 407/568–2885. $11.50 adults, $9.50 seniors over 60 and children ages 3–11, children under 3 free. Open daily 9–6.*
Worth-It Rating ★★★

MIDWAY AIRBOAT RIDES Skim across the saw grass in a high-speed airboat while spotting cranes, egrets, eagles, and other local wildlife—perhaps even a gator or a water moccasin. Trips from Florida's oldest fish camp, on the Banana River, last 35 to 45 minutes. It's buggy and hot in summer, raw and windy in winter. *28501 E. Route 50, Christmas, tel. 407/568–6790. $12 adults, $6 children ages 2–12, children under 2 free. Open daily 9–4:45.*

Worth-It Rating ★★★★★ Subtract 2 if swamps give you the creeps.

chapter 17

BEACH, BEACH, BEACH
Florida's Atlantic Beaches

O rlando is only about an hour's drive from the beach towns of Florida's East Coast, and each one has a unique flavor. Some permit driving on the sand—catching rays next to the sand roadway can take some getting used to, so choose accordingly.

DAYTONA BEACH AND NORTH

DAYTONA BEACH At the turn of the century, people raced their cars on the hard-packed white sand at Daytona, about an hour northeast of Orlando and, because of the good highway access, one of the easiest beaches to get to. Since then, driving on the beach has been a distinguishing feature of Daytona life, though beach traffic has been severely reduced during the past year by successful protests from environmental groups fighting for the protection of endangered sea turtles. The result is that most of the Volusia Beaches, including large portions of Daytona and New Smyrna, are now closed to vehicular traffic.

Where you still find cars it's still dangerous—occasionally, an errant car does run over a pedestrian or two—but traffic is kept to a crawl and restricted to designated lanes, and handy motorized carts offer snacks, sodas, and even sand castle–building aids, and rent beach umbrellas, boogie-boards, and motor scooters. The surf is moderate, with prime East Coast waves. Surf-fishing is allowed in the early morning and away from bathers. There is also good fishing on the nearby Halifax River, and you'll find plenty of deep-sea charters. To the south, **Ponce Inlet** affords spectacular fishing from shore, pier, or boat. The historic red **Ponce de León Lighthouse** makes a pleasant focal point of an outing, and several local seafood restaurants nearby serve fresh, authentic Florida fare such as shrimp, oysters, scallops, mahi-mahi, and my favorite native fish, grouper. You'll also find native Florida lobster; it has no claws and it's a lot chewier than Maine lobster, but some people actually prefer it.

Tens of thousands of college students flock to Daytona for spring break. So between February and May, you may have trouble finding a room, and when you do, you may find yourself sandwiched between rowdy drinking parties. The spring break reputation has made Daytona the place to see hard bodies in skimpy bathing suits the rest of the year, too.

The **Daytona International Speedway** (1801 W. International Speedway, tel. 904/254–2700) is another major player in town. Its biggest annual events are **Bike Week**, a celebration of motorcycle racing in early March, and the **Daytona**

500 auto race in February. The speedway's new **Daytona USA** includes a simulated ride in a stock car race and a racing museum. It's a must-see only for serious enthusiasts.

Because the speedway dominates local politics and because its most successful races are motorcycle events, Daytona has rolled out the red carpet for America's motorcycle gangs. Establishments offering adult entertainment, tattooing, and body-piercing have become ubiquitous. Although this makes some families uncomfortable, there has been no noticeable increase in the kinds of crimes normally associated with bikers.

Spring breakers and bikers are hard on hotels, and most of Daytona's beachfront shows the wear and tear. Never get a room here without seeing it first. Still, Daytona has some lovely places to stay, including the new **Marriott** (100 N. Atlantic Ave., tel. 904/254–8200) and the **Adam's Mark Resort** (2637 S. Atlantic Ave., tel. 904/767–7350).

Information: Convention & Visitors Bureau of Daytona Beach, 126 E. Orange Ave., Daytona Beach, 32114-4406, tel. 904/255–0415. Destination Daytona, 1801 Volusia Ave., Daytona Beach 32114, tel. 904/253–8669.

Worth-It Rating ★★★ Add 1 if you're a race fan, 2 if you're a NASCAR card–carrier.

ORMOND BEACH Immediately north of and adjacent to Daytona, Ormond is Daytona without many of the problems—at least for the moment. Ormond is quieter and easier to get around in than its neighbor—except during spring break, race weeks, and bike week. During those times, Daytona has no city limits. Though Ormond has its mom-and-pop motels, most properties here are more upscale.

Information: Chamber of Commerce, 165 W. Granada Blvd., Ormond Beach, 32174-6303, tel. 904/677-3454.

Worth-It Rating ★★★★

ST. AUGUSTINE An hour north of Daytona is the oldest city in the United States and one of Florida's best family destinations—educational, inexpensive, and fun. The St. Augustine slogan says it all: "Eight miles of beach and the rest is history." The history begins in 1513, when Juan Ponce de León landed nearby and claimed his discovery for the Spanish king. Formally established by Pedro Menendez de Aviles in 1565 on Mantanzas Bay, St. Augustine is one of the oldest continuously incorporated cities in North America, though it has flown the Spanish, British, U.S., and Confederate flags. The site of de Aviles's landing is also the site of the country's oldest church, the **Mission Nombre di Dios** (San Marco and Ocean Aves., tel. 904/824-2809). St. Augustine is loaded with things to see and do, most accessible via two trams that let you get on and off at will.

One of the best-known sites in St. Augustine is Florida's oldest fort, the impregnable **Castillo de San Marcos** (Canal St.)—cannonballs simply sank into the spongy local coquina rock of which it was built. The original **Ripley's Believe It Or Not Museum** (19 San Marco Ave.) is also in St. Augustine, along with **Zorayda Castle** (83 King St.), a fortress built by a paranoid father to imprison his maiden daughters, and **Potter's Wax Museum** (17 King St.), an eerie collection of lifelike wax figures. There are also restorations of a home, store, and jail, and, on U.S. A1A, the world-famous **St. Augustine Alligator Farm** (999 Anastasia Blvd.), which features reptile and other wildlife shows and exhibits and is very similar to Gatorland. (I recommend that you see an alligator farm while you're in Florida, but you certainly don't need to visit more than one.)

My son Ricky's pick is the **Museum of Weapons and Early American History** (21 King St.), the life work of weapons collector Donna Lee Walton. Displaying weapons dating back to the Colonial period, this little building is simply packed with Colonial and Civil War memorabilia. Tiffany, my daughter, favors the **Oldest Wooden School House** (14 St. George St.), built in the 1700s with floors of tabby, a mortar made of indigenous oyster shell. The **Lightner Museum** (75 King St.), housed in a former hotel that's now a part of downtown St. Augustine's Flagler College, is Terrie's pick. St. Augustine came into a golden age at the turn of the last century, when railroad tycoon Henry Flagler made the city the number one tourist destination in the United States. The Lightner Museum displays the world's premier collection of Louis Comfort Tiffany stained glass and other art and artifacts of that grand era.

Another of my favorite St. Augustine destinations is **O. C. White's Restaurant** (118 Av. Menendez, tel. 904/824–0808), in an 18th-century structure reputed to have been a pirate's residence. Owner David White regales diners with tales of the home's notorious past and of its current ghostly residents (featured on TV's *Sightings*). We all love the family-priced seafood. At the other end of the historic bayfront, anchored by the Castillo de San Marcos on the north, is the restored **King's Forge Restaurant** (12 Av. Menendez, tel. 904/829–1488). Swords, antique guns, and armor adorn the walls of the building where an 18th-century blacksmith toiled. You can dine on seafood, steak, and prime rib, while enjoying the best view in town, a spectacular panorama of Castillo de San Marcos and Matanzas Bay.

BEACH, BEACH, BEACH

Also in St. Augustine is the official Florida state play, *The Cross and Sword* (1 Riberia St.), a spectacular dramatization of the early struggles for control of the area, performed in an amphitheater carved out of the palmetto-scrub jungle. Bring mosquito repellent.

St. Augustine's best beach is on beautiful **Anastasia Island.** You can drive on some stretches of it, but the nicest parts are accessible only on foot. The surf is moderate and the beach composed of rare coquina—tiny, pulverized shells mixed with dark sand. Another good beach is on a small barrier island south of St. Augustine near Marineland, a venerable Florida oceanside attraction (*see* Chapter 15); it's the site of the clean, pleasant **Marineland of Florida Quality Inn** (101 U.S. A1A, Marineland 32804, tel. 904/471–1222). Old hotels, vintage B&Bs, and chain hostelries abound.

Information: Visitor Information Center, 1 Riberia St., St. Augustine, 32084, tel. 904/825–1000; www.oldcity.com.
Worth-It Rating ★★★★★

SOUTH OF DAYTONA

NEW SMYRNA BEACH The Namey family condo is immediately south of Daytona at this quiet, secluded beach. The place stays quiet because there are no major four-lane roads from Orlando. Hotels are few and small—among them the **Holiday Inn Hotel Suites** (1401 S. Atlantic Ave., New Smyrna Beach, 32169-3113, tel. 904/426–0020) and the **Islander Beach Resort** (1601 S. Atlantic Ave., New Smyrna Beach, 32169-3199, tel. 904/427–3452). Instead, most people stay in individual condos or rentals such as the legendary

Roberto del Mar (3619 Hill St., New Smyrna Beach 32169, tel. 407/644–3292). To the south is the northern end of the **Canaveral National Seashore** (tel. 407/867–2805), part of the buffer zone around the Space Center and the site of the last totally unspoiled Florida beach. Here, we have petted manatees, watched dolphins frolic, and picked giant conch right off the sandy shore. I sincerely hope I'm not making the area sound too appealing. We would just as soon keep this off-the-beaten-path secret to ourselves.

Information: Chamber of Commerce, 115 Canal St., New Smyrna Beach, 32168-7003, tel. 904/428-2449. New Smyrna Beach Rentals, 4155 S. Atlantic Ave., Suite 509, New Smyrna Beach, 32169-3793, tel. 800/609–7874.

Worth-It Rating ★★★★

COCOA AND THE SPACE COAST This is probably your best value on the East Coast. Easily accessible by the Beeline Expressway or via Route 50 east of Orlando, the beaches of Brevard County, known as the Space Coast, are family-friendly, safe, and reasonably priced. Many are part of the southern end of the Canaveral National Seashore. A Space Coast visit can be combined with visits to the Space Center and surrounding attractions (*see* Chapter 16).

Florida's biggest surfing waves are nearby, at the **Canaveral Jetties** north of Cocoa Beach. Brevard beaches have soft, white sand, with occasional patches of coquina. Driving is not allowed, but there are beach concessions and oceanfront restaurants. (Be aware that a state law makes it mandatory for all such establishments to continuously play Jimmy Buffett's "Margaritaville." If you find a beach bar that is not playing the song, report it immediately to the local authorities.)

The centerpiece of Cocoa Beach is **Ron Jon's Surf Shop** (4151 N. Atlantic Ave., tel. 407/799–8820), the largest surf shop in the world—actually a whole shopping complex occupying several city blocks, with sections specializing in everything aquatic. In the main store, a three-story waterfall runs through an atrium and you'll find the largest selection of T-shirts anywhere. (That's what it feels like, anyway.) Ron Jon's blankets Orlando with more outdoor advertising than even Universal Studios Escape. Check it out.

Along Atlantic Avenue is a favorite family eating spot, **Yen-Yen** (2 N. Atlantic Ave., tel. 407/783–9512), which serves Hong Kong–style cuisine. And we often travel the 50 minutes east to Titusville from Orlando to stand in line at the popular **Dixie Crossroads** (1475 Garden St., tel. 407/268–5000) for all-you-can-eat Florida rock shrimp—they're split, broiled, and served hot, like tiny lobsters. It's not uncommon to spy an astronaut here.

At the north end of the Space Coast, north of Cocoa, is **Playalinda Beach.** It is part of the Canaveral National Seashore (although it is not connected by land to the section south of New Smyrna Beach). Playalinda often has nude or topless bathing, though its status changes with the complexion of local politics.

If you want to stay in the area, try the **Radisson Suite Hotel Oceanfront** (3101 N. U.S. A1A, Indialantic, 32903-2135, tel. 407/773–9260); the **Holiday Inn** (1300 N. Atlantic Ave., Cocoa Beach, 32931-3299, tel. 407/783–2271); the **Ramada Inn–Kennedy Space Center** (900 Friday Rd., Cocoa, 32926-3313, tel. 407/631–1210); the **Ramada Oceanfront Resort Hotel** (1035 U.S. A1A, Satellite Beach, 32937-2320, tel. 407/777–7200); or the **Ramada Inn Kennedy Space Center** (3500 Cheney Hwy., Titusville, 32780-2503, tel. 407/269–5510).

SOUTH OF DAYTONA

Information: *Chamber of Commerce, 400 Fortenberry Rd., Merritt Island 32952, tel. 407/459–2200. Welcome Center, 1325 N. Atlantic Ave., Cocoa Beach, 32931-3220, tel. 407/783–8811. Chamber of Commerce, 1005 E. Strawbridge Ave., Melbourne, 32901-4740, tel. 407/724–5400.*

Worth-It Rating ★★★★ Add 1 if you combine a visit here with a trip to the Space Center.

chapter 18

SHOPPERTOONITIES

I n no other place in the world do you have more opportunities to buy more things bearing the likeness of Mickey Mouse. Still, although you can save money on many items by shopping outside the parks, there are many items you won't find elsewhere. This is particularly true of items themed around beloved characters like E.T., Fievel, and Shamu, which are not widely distributed outside the parks that feature them. And remember, there's a lot more to Central Florida than characters. So many people from abroad go on shopping sprees here that export specialists have sprung up, selling everything from Levis to electronics. Read on for some of my favorite shopping destinations—all open daily.

MY SHORT LIST

★★★★★

SPORTS DOMINATOR I have regularly seen shoes by the top brands like Reebok at this high-volume outlet for as little as $9.95 a pair. While I can't guarantee what they'll have when you arrive, I can promise consistently amazing prices—even on official uniforms of home teams everywhere. *6464 International Dr., Orlando, tel. 407/354–2100; 8550 International Dr., Orlando, tel. 407/345–0110; 7550 W. Irlo Bronson Memorial Hwy., Kissimmee, tel. 407/397–4700.*

BARGAIN WORLD Some of the largest souvenir shops around, these have a gazillion T-shirts, toys, and trinkets as well as film, sunscreen, and even jackets—all at incredibly low prices. *6464 International Dr., Orlando, tel. 407/351–0900; 8520 International Dr., Orlando, tel. 407/352–0214; 7586 W. Irlo Bronson Memorial Hwy., Kissimmee, tel. 407/239–7733; 5781 W. Irlo Bronson Memorial Hwy., Kissimmee, tel. 407/239–0077.*

ASTRONAUT HALL OF FAME Know some kids who have seen *Apollo 13* 13 times? Here at the main entrance to the Space Center, they'll find the best selection of space-related merchandise anywhere: patches, decals, medallions, astronaut suits, model rockets, and more. *6225 Vectorspace Blvd., Titusville, tel. 407/269–6100.*

GATORLAND Yes, Gatorland. Although primarily known as an attraction, it is also one of the world's largest commercial alligator farms and sells great alligator shoes, boots, belts, wallets, and luggage at farm-direct prices. *14501 S. Orange Blossom Trail, Orlando, tel. 407/855–5496.*

RON JON SURF SHOP The world's largest surf shop, open around the clock, is a multi-block complex, announced by more billboards than even Universal Studios Escape. Check out the three-story waterfall in the lobby, the world's largest selection of T-shirts, and surf gear, swimwear, and exotic gifts galore. *4151 N. Atlantic Ave., Cocoa Beach, tel. 407/799–8820.*

WORLD OF DENIM At these huge Levis and casual-wear dealers, volume keeps prices phenomenally low, and many people come to Orlando annually to stock up. *1411 Sand Lake Rd., Orlando, tel. 407/851–1773; 8255 International Dr., Orlando, tel. 407/345–0263.*

SHOPPING CENTERS, DISCOUNT MALLS

POINTE ORLANDO You can't miss the four-story teddy bear in front of FAO Schwarz, which includes complete shops devoted entirely to Lego and Barbie. But Pointe Orlando is much more than that. There's an awesome example of the next generation of movie theaters, as well as over 70 terrific stores and eateries. *9101 International Dr., Orlando, tel. 407/248–2838.*
Worth-It Rating ★★★★★

BELZ FACTORY OUTLET WORLD This enormous complex right on I-Drive is two separate major malls with four smaller annexes. Remember O. J. Simpson's famous Bruno Magli shoes? One of the few places you can get them is here, along with stuff from other designers and shoemakers; Polly Flinders, Fieldcrest/Cannon, Fitz & Floyd, Mikasa, and

others are represented, and prices are up to 75% off retail. *4949 International Dr., Orlando, tel. 407/352–7110.*
Worth-It Rating ★★★★★

QUALITY OUTLET CENTER Although this mall is not as complete as Belz, the Adidas, Great Western Boot, Florsheim, and Laura Ashley here are the only ones in the attractions area. *5437 International Dr. at Sand Lake Rd., Orlando, tel. 407/423–5885.*
Worth-It Rating ★★★★

FESTIVAL CENTERS

At these themed shopping centers, the entertainment value is high and the retail experience is offbeat and unique. Some have street entertainers or rides and activities for children. The shops are usually one-of-a-kind stores where you're greeted personally by the owners.

CHURCH STREET MARKET This is just across the courtyard from Church Street Station, and if you didn't know the politics of the place, you'd think it was part of the same complex. Actually, it was cleverly created by another developer to cash in on Church Street's popularity and its advertising. Still, it has a number of worthwhile shoppertoonities, including a **Sharper Image** and **Brookstone's**. For food, there's the politically incorrect **Hooter's**, a sports bar, featuring spicy chicken wings served by scantily clad young women, and **Jungle Jim's**, with a cute jungle theme the kids will love, and family-friendly prices. *55 W. Church St., Orlando, tel. 407/872–3500.*

Worth-It Rating ★★★★ Deduct 1 if you have to make a special trip.

CHURCH STREET EXCHANGE This is the shopping part of Church Street Station, with over 50 specialty stores, many of them locally owned and operated. A flight-ready biplane hangs from the ceiling on the second floor, where there's also an excellent food court and **Commander Ragtime's Midway,** possibly Orlando's most extensive arcade, with about a zillion video games and claw machines. The fabulous **Buffalo Trading Company** has all kinds of Western items including many, many fringed buckskin jackets. The **Bumby Emporium,** also huge, sells Church Street souvenirs and lots of old-timey stuff. *55 W. Church St., Orlando, tel. 407/872–3500.*
Worth-It Rating ★★★★★

MERCADO The Mediterranean-themed Mercado invites you to eat! shop! and party! The 60 festive shops include at least several that may well be unduplicated, including **Space 2000,** loaded with space souvenirs; **Conch Republic,** which caters to fans of Florida's own Jimmy Buffett; and my son's favorite, **U-Spy,** a whole store full of honest-to-gosh James Bond–type spy gear. Mercado is also home to **Blazing Pianos,** a nightclub featuring a pair of rock & rollers on dueling grand pianos. Talk about great balls of fire! *8445 International Dr., Orlando, tel. 407/345–9337.*
Worth-It Rating ★★★★★ Subtract 1 if you're not staying on I-Drive or if you're not eating.

chapter 19

SLEEPING BEAUTIES

A Florida state law requires each household to offer free accommodations to all friends, relatives, acquaintances, and acquaintances of acquaintances who pass through town. That's just a joke. But the truth is that despite the 100,000 hotel rooms around town (more than in almost any other city in the world) and despite the rock-bottom-budget prices of many of them, most locals maintain a guest room for both invited and uninvited visitors.

Since our family already has our quota of visiting out-of-towners, I'm going to give you the next best thing—the very best hotel values around town. First I'll give you my short list, my absolute favorites. Then I'll give you a range of other good bets for each of the several major lodging areas.

Why do you need my recommendations? When I started Visitor Information Television, I called on nearly every hotel and motel in the area to try to get them to carry our channel.

I have visited every one of the properties listed here again and again over the years. Hopefully, as a result, I know a few things that you don't. For instance:

- Florida swamps breed mosquitoes the size of butterflies and cockroaches the size of golf balls. If your motel was built over a swamp, as many properties were, the only way to keep the bugs under control is with chemicals. I have been in rooms that made my nose burn and my eyes turn blood red. I left those places off the list.
- Some tourist traps are seedy, sleazy, and just plain dirty. *They* won't tell you just how bad they are when you make reservations.
- Most resorts advertise in the local tourist publications. Many post rates daily on electric signs. Because I live and work here, I read the same publications and see the same signs that you will—but all the time. I have tried to include the places that regularly post the lowest rates and deliver the best value in each area, in each price category.

As I noted previously, access to transportation and ticket deals is important in determining the overall hotel value. Disney's on-property hotels have direct access to Disney transportation, an extra that's worth money. The resorts that have banded together with Universal Studios, Sea World, and Wet 'n Wild—all covered below—also provide complimentary transportation and special packages that include tickets. In choosing either a Disney or an Orlando resort, it is best to shop around for the best available package.

I've called this chapter "Sleeping Beauties" because here in Orlando your hotel will be an especially important part of the overall vacation experience, and the number of theme properties is increasing. I've included them all, along with a good selection of those that stand out from the crowd and offer significant extra value, particularly when the prices are competitive. Not every place that didn't make my list is a flea bag or a toxic dump. Some were omitted just because I don't know them personally, others because I didn't think they delivered value equal to their rates. The ones I did include I can recommend without reservation. Information about the facilities follows my comments. Unless I tell you otherwise, all properties have an arcade with video games, at least one swimming pool, a no-pets-allowed policy, and transportation to and from some major area attractions (noted below when it's free).

If you're traveling with your kids, be on the lookout for "baby-sitting adventures"—that is, child-care with a theme, in a themed environment and often with costumed characters. They're usually available both day and night.

PRICE CATEGORIES Dollar-sign symbols indicate regular nightly rates for two people in a room (called rack rates in the hospitality industry):

Budget	$	under $49
Moderate	$$	$49–$99
Upscale	$$$	$99 and up

MAIN ATTRACTIONS AREAS Hotels in and around Orlando are clustered in three main areas:

International Drive Universal Studios Escape is on the north end of this busy strip, Sea World on the south. It's also home to the Orlando Convention Center, Wet 'n Wild, and several smaller attractions. There are more rooms and places to eat here than in any other area.

Lake Buena Vista This is the area around Route 535 at I–4 Exit 27, near Downtown Disney; it's convenient to Disney attractions.

The U.S. 192 Corridor in Kissimmee Also known as the Irlo Bronson Memorial Highway, the strip begins at the end of Disney property near the Magic Kingdom and Celebration, the new Disney planned community. It is close to Water Mania, Medieval Times, Old Town, Wild Bill's, and other sites. This is also where you'll find some of the area's lowest room rates. Parts of the area are also known as Maingate, because of their proximity to the main gate to the Magic Kingdom back when the Magic Kingdom was all there was to Walt Disney World. In downtown Kissimmee, U.S. 192 is known as Vine Street. Most of the time, it reminds me of a Hollywood movie set, all front with no back. Kissimmee/Osceola County is one of America's largest cattle-producing areas. Check it out: Just a few feet behind the strip, cows still graze.

Downtown Disney and Other Areas Inside WDW On Walt Disney World property, some hotels are owned by Disney, some are not. The Disney-owned properties tend to be high-end; rooms tend to be small at those that are moderately priced or in the budget categories—not a problem if your group numbers four or fewer. Almost all hotels have terrific theme swimming pools and almost all are on lakes. They may have a beach and there's almost always a marina where you can rent zippy little speedboats called Water Sprites as well as other craft. Transportation around WDW is always free.

Hotels that are not Disney-owned are clustered in Downtown Disney in an area that used to be known as Hotel Plaza. These represent an exceptional value, and guests enjoy many of the perks available to those staying at WDW-owned hotels, including free transportation between hotels and Disney attractions, guaranteed admission to Disney theme parks during normal park operating hours (even on "sold-out" days), and preferential treatment when you want to book tee times on Walt Disney World championship golf courses. The Marketplace at Downtown Disney is within walking distance, and from there you can catch a bus to almost any other WDW destination.

If you are considering a hotel outside WDW that I haven't recommended, choose carefully: Base your decision only on recent personal visits by someone you trust, since there has been a lot of decline among some U.S. 192 properties in the last year or so, and a few sections of the strip are downright unwelcoming. Be sure to get the exact location of the property (or look it up on a map). And don't be misled by names. Some properties add the name of an area to its own (i.e. Maingate, Lake Buena Vista) in an effort to make you think they're closer than they are to the area in question. For instance, several hotels that have called themselves Orlando North (not on my list) are really in Maitland and Altamonte. That's 35 miles north of Disney property, or about an hour by car in morning rush-hour traffic.

Note that I don't recommend downtown Orlando or, unless you're specifically looking for adult entertainment, the South Orange Blossom Trail (U.S. 441, known around town as the South Trail or SOBT).

My Short List

★★★★★

The following are my favorite hotels in Orlando, with the least expensive first.

COMFORT INN LAKE BUENA VISTA This relatively new complex, with four five-story buildings, is very clean and well maintained. Convenient to Downtown Disney, it's visible from I–4; transportation to and from WDW attractions is complimentary. Kids under 11 with parents eat free, and there are two heated swimming pools. *8442 Palm Pkwy., Orlando 32836, tel. 407/239–7300 or 800/999–7300. 640 rooms. Restaurant, bar. Pets accepted. $–$$*

RODEWAY INTERNATIONAL INN This simple, clean I-Drive motel with all the basics usually posts the area's lowest rates. The restaurant serves buffet-style, and there's a Japanese steak house. *6327 International Dr., Orlando 32819, tel. 407/351–4444 or 800/999–6327. 315 rooms. 2 restaurants, bar, supervised children's program (summer only). Pets accepted. $–$$*

DISNEY'S ALL-STAR RESORTS These resorts in the southwest corner of the property near Blizzard Beach and Downtown Disney are the best of the moderately priced properties at Walt Disney World. It's hard to beat the rates anywhere. The **All-Star Sports Resort** can be recognized by its giant football helmet, immense basketball, and other sports-equipment sculptures. The **All-Star Music Resort** features a giant guitar, huge piano, and jumbo jukebox. The **All-Star Movie Resort** is scheduled to open in July 1999. The swimming pools (there are four in the complex) are like mini water parks on the same themes. Staying at these resorts gets you all Disney privileges, including unlimited free Disney transportation. It almost doesn't matter that the rooms are a little small. *WDW Central Reservations, Box 10100, Lake Buena Vista 32830, tel. 407/934–7639 or 407/824–3000. 5,760 rooms. Food court, bakery, 2 bars, hot tub, baby-sitting. $$*

HOLIDAY INN MAINGATE EAST I rate this property one of the best on U.S. 192 in its price range. Even among Orlando hotels, most of which are family-friendly, this one stands out. Free child care at varying times, and kids 12 and under eat free with their parents in the restaurant. You can't get any better than that. There are two swimming pools. *5678 W. Irlo Bronson Memorial Hwy., Kissimmee 34746, tel. 407/396–4488 or 800/FON–KIDS. 614 rooms, 55 kids' suites. 1 restaurant, 1 food court, 1 bar, kitchenettes, health club, 2 hot tubs, lighted tennis court, baby-sitting, supervised children's program, playground. Pets accepted. $$*

CARIBE ROYALE RESORT SUITES Lush landscaping, waterfalls, and a moat mark one of the most impressive layouts in town. A 75-foot water slide passes over the waterfalls into the enormous free-form pool. Nearby is a children's wading pool with aim-and-squirt water cannons. The playground is modern and full of climbing things, tunnels, and slides. All accommodations are in one-bedroom suites and two-bedroom villas, which sleep 6 to 10 and have fully equipped kitchens. The living rooms have sofa beds, wet bars, microwaves, and refrigerators. Breakfast is free, and so is transportation to and from Disney. When you figure in the money you can save by occasionally eating in your room, you could save money at this deluxe resort. *14300 International Dr. Orlando 32821, tel. 407/238–8000 or 800/823–8300. 1,200 suites, 120 villas. 2 restaurants, bar, pool bar, deli, hot tubs, 2 exercise rooms. $$$*

THE CASTLE, DOUBLETREE RESORT Why stay in a hotel when you can stay in a castle? When hotelier Richard Kessler's young daughter asked her daddy why she couldn't stay in the Cinderella Castle, Kessler got the idea to build this magnificent medieval-style property, which dominates the International Drive skyline. The attention to detail is awesome—there are intricate mosaics, fantasy medieval art, and special effects everywhere, even in-room sound effects (I like the ocean sounds). A medieval fountain with three giant bronze fish spouts at the center of the spacious round pool. The gift shop offers medieval collectibles, and the hotel is home to the eclectic Café Tu-Tu Tango and Vito's Chop House, both of which are excellent. There's free transportation to both Disney and Orlando FlexTicket attractions. *8629 International Dr., Orlando 32819, tel. 800/95–CASTLE or 407/345–1511, fax 407/248–8181. 216 rooms, 7 suites. 2 restaurants, 2 bars, hot tub. $$$*

CLARION PLAZA HOTEL This really nice 12-story hotel right in the middle of things on I-Drive, near the convention center, is very pretty, with a wonderful big pool and a spacious patio that never seems overcrowded; you can usually find a chair. The grounds are attractively landscaped and the lobby is huge. The food in the restaurant is excellent. With lots of facilities for the money, it's a wallet-pleaser as well. When reserving, check to see whether there will be a major convention there during your stay; if so, you should probably go elsewhere. *9700 International Dr., Orlando 32819-8114, tel. 407/352–9700 or 800/627–8258. 810 rooms, 32 suites. 2 restaurants, 2 bars, baby-sitting. $$$*

DISNEY'S FORT WILDERNESS RESORT AND CAMPGROUND

At Tiffany's request, we spent her fourth birthday at this lakeside WDW campground and we had a great time. You'll find all the traditional camp activities: campfire sing-alongs (Chip and Dale show up), marshmallow roasts, and outdoor movies (some not screened anywhere else in the world). Don't let the campground idea keep you away if you're not a camper. Besides the tent and RV sites, you can rent suite-size digs with full kitchens in spiffy free-standing manufactured homes (like deluxe RVs on foundations)—and you'll pay about the same as you would for a regular room elsewhere in WDW. Plus, there are three swimming pools and loads of other facilities: horseback riding, fishing, and nature trails. The campground is right next to River Country, and Disney transportation is free. *WDW Central Reservations, Box 10100, Lake Buena Vista 32830, tel. 407/934–7639. 408 rooms, 387 RV sites, 390 tent sites. 2 restaurants, bar, lighted tennis court, baby-sitting, playground. $$$*

DOUBLETREE GUEST SUITES AT DOWNTOWN DISNEY

This is the best pick on Disney property for families who need a lot of space at a reasonable price. Little touches abound, like the hot cookies on arrival and a children's registration area to entertain and occupy the little ones during check-in and check-out. My editor stayed here with her extended family and said that the vacation worked because of the accommodations here: each is a spacious suite that includes a living room with a TV, Sony PlayStation, and a double sleep sofa, plus either one bedroom (in units that sleep six) or two bedrooms (in those that accommodate ten); each bedroom has two double beds or a king bed and a TV. (Even the bathrooms have their own TVs.) There's a Disney store and free continuous transportation to and from WDW. For all this, the price is right—not too much more than at Disney's own bottom-of-the-line properties, which sleep just four to a room. *2305 Hotel Plaza Blvd., Lake Buena Vista 32830, tel. 407/934–1000. 229 suites. Restaurant, hot tub, 2 lighted tennis courts, volleyball court, playground. $$$*

THE GRAND FLORIDIAN RESORT AND SPA

At Disney, you can't do better than this stately white re-creation of a turn-of-the-century resort with a vintage white Rolls-Royce out front. Overlooking the Seven Seas Lagoon, directly opposite the Magic Kingdom, it's incredibly convenient. And the view of the Magic Kingdom fireworks across the lake is breathtaking—as is the view of the splendid nightly Electrical Water Pageant. *WDW Central Reservations, Box 10100, Lake Buena Vista 32830, tel. 407/824–3000. 900 rooms and suites. 6 restaurants, 3 bars, health club, hot tub, beach, boat rentals, golf, lighted tennis court, baby-sitting. $$$*

LOEWS PORTOFINO BAY AT UNIVERSAL STUDIOS ESCAPE

Guest-service representatives greet you curbside, handle your luggage, your car, and your check-in at the ultimate luxury theme-park resort. Smart Rooms remember your thermostat setting and alert housekeeping when your room is vacant. In one of the 26 top-of-the-line Villa Rooms, your butler will unpack for you and prepare fresh orange juice every morning. Special guest privileges include early admission to Universal Studios Escape and a room key that can be used as a credit card in the Universal parks. Complimentary transportation includes a gondola ride along the picturesque waterway into the theme parks. *1000 Universal Studios Plaza, Orlando 32819-7610, tel. 407/363–8000 or 800/235–6397. 750 rooms, 26 villas. 8 restaurants, 3 bars, pool with water slide, 3 hot tubs, spa and fitness center, baby-sitting, children's play area and supervised children's program. $$$*

MARRIOTT'S ORLANDO WORLD CENTER

This gorgeous high-rise is the best hotel not only in the Lake Buena Vista area but in all Orlando. General Manager Jim McDonnell runs the tightest ship in town. You can't miss it—it's the area's tallest structure, and it's near Epcot's main entrance. From higher floors you can get the clearest aerial view anywhere of all three parks. Of the five pools, the free-form pool is the best, with waterfalls and a water slide. Because the hotel will be undergoing extensive renovations through 2000, call regarding amenities, as some may be unavailable. *8701 World Center Dr., Orlando 32821, tel. 407/239–4200 or 800/228–9290. 1,503 rooms. 6 restaurants, 2 bars, health club, 3 hot tubs, baby-sitting, supervised children's program, Lollipop Lounge for kids 4–12, playground. $$$*

OMNI ROSEN

The signature property of local hotelier Harris Rosen is the most luxurious hotel on I-Drive. The rooms are large, and the beds, pillows, and towels are oversized and fluffy; everything is flawlessly maintained. The heated pool is jumbo. *9840 International Dr., Orlando 32819, tel. 407/354–9840 or 800/627–8258. 1,334 rooms, 89 suites. 3 restaurants, 2 bars, health club, 3 hot tubs, lighted tennis court, baby-sitting. $$$*

RADISSON TWIN TOWERS HOTEL The largest Radisson hotel on earth, at the entrance to Universal Studios, is also one of the nicest, with modern, spacious rooms. Proximity to the park makes it a frequent choice of visiting celebrities. In fact, you can't get much closer. *5780 Major Blvd., Orlando 32819, tel. 407/351–1000 or 800/333–3333. 740 rooms, 5 suites. Restaurant, 3 bars, health club, hot tub, baby-sitting, playground. $$$*

THE WYNDHAM PALACE RESORT AND SPA This towering structure is almost as tall as Marriott's Orlando World Center, and the lounge on top and the west-facing rooms above the ninth floor have a clear and close-up view of the nightly pyrotechnics in the Magic Kingdom, Epcot, Disney–MGM, and Pleasure Island. Of all the Downtown Disney properties, the Buena Vista is the closest to the theme parks, so if you use the hotel transportation you'll be the last on and the first off. It's also the most luxurious property. It has three heated swimming pools, volleyball, jogging trails, and a large, serious spa with complete facilities. The complex includes a concierge floor, several no-smoking "Evergreen Rooms" designed to remain odor-free, and an adjacent complex of one- and two-bedroom suites. And all rooms and suites have a balcony or patio. Arthur's 27 is known as one of the area's finest restaurants—it also has the fireworks view—and the Laughing Kookaburra is a top hangout for the local party kids. *1900 Buena Vista Dr., Lake Buena Vista 32830, tel. 407/827–2727 or 800/327–2990. 984 rooms, 30 suites. 5 restaurants, 4 bars, hot tub, 3 lighted tennis courts, supervised children's program, playground. $$$*

Other Good Bets

These hotels and motels offer good value-for-dollar, and I recommend them wholeheartedly. Many are perfectly wonderful, and I've given them my highest rating, but for whatever reason, they just aren't extra-special *to me* personally and I haven't put them on my short list. You may well feel otherwise.

INTERNATIONAL DRIVE AREA: UNIVERSAL CITY RESORTS

The following properties offer free transportation to Universal, Sea World, and Wet 'n Wild and many sell discount vacation packages that include the Orlando FlexTicket. For more information and the latest rates, call Universal City Travel at 800/711–0080.

HOLIDAY INN HOTEL SUITES UNIVERSAL STUDIOS There's a special pool for kids. *5905 Kirkman Rd., Orlando 32819, tel. 407/351–3333. 393 rooms. Restaurant, bar. $$*
Worth-It Rating ★★★★

LAS PALMAS HOTEL This is a good basic choice that's an especially good deal on Universal City Travel packages. It's secure, with inside-entrance rooms, and it's got a great location on International Drive, directly across from Wet 'n Wild and just a couple of minutes from Universal Studios. *6233 International Dr., Orlando 32819, tel. 407/351–3900. 262 rooms. Restaurant, bar. $$*
Worth-It Rating ★★★★

COMFORT SUITES OF ORLANDO You can get a suite with a microwave and fridge for the price of a budget room here; the one-bedroom suites sleep up to five. The pool complex includes a wading pool, and the location is just 2 miles from Universal Studios. *9350 Turkey Lake Rd., Orlando 32819, tel. 407/351–5050 or 800/228–8150. 214 Suites. Restaurant, bar, hot tub, playground. $$–$$$*
Worth-It Rating ★★★★

DELTA ORLANDO RESORT MAINGATE This 25-acre resort has large grounds, with well-planned and well-maintained recreational areas, including three swimming pools, two wading pools, and miniature golf. *5715 Major Blvd., Orlando 32819-7988, tel. 407/351–3340. 800 rooms. 3 restaurants, bar, 3 hot tubs, saunas, 2 lighted tennis courts, volleyball beach, teen center and lounge, supervised children's program, playground. Pets accepted. $$$*
Worth-It Rating ★★★★

EMBASSY SUITES Less than five minutes' drive from Universal is this excellent example of Embassy's consistently high quality. Every unit is a suite that sleeps up to six in its bedroom and sofa-bedded living room; there's always a wet bar, refrigerator, microwave oven, and two TVs. Breakfast is cooked to order—and it's free. This is a bit nicer than the Comfort Suites, but more expensive. *8250 Jamaican Ct., Orlando 32819, tel. 407/345–8250 or 800/327–9797. 26 suites. Bar, health club, hot tub. $$$*
Worth-It Rating ★★★★

OTHER GOOD BETS

HILTON GRAND VACATIONS CLUB Grand Vacations is Hilton's time-share division, but you don't have to own to stay in this one right next to Sea World, minutes away from Universal Studios. Rooms are very big and nicely appointed—they even have chandeliers. *6878 Sea Harbor Dr., Orlando 32821, tel. 407/239–0100 or 800/448–2736. 500 rooms. Restaurant, bar, health club, 4 hot tubs, shuffleboard, supervised children's activities, playground. $$$*
Worth-It Rating ★★★★

OTHER I-DRIVE RESORTS

QUALITY INN INTERNATIONAL Proof that not all motels are created equal, this Quality Inn has clean, spacious rooms and two heated swimming pools, as well as rates that are consistently some of the strip's lowest. Kids 11 and under with paying adults eat free at the restaurant's all-you-can-eat breakfast and dinner buffets; Mickey D's, the world's largest McDonald's, is next door. *7600 International Dr., Orlando 32819, tel. 407/351–1600 or 800/875–7600. 728 rooms. Restaurant, bar. Pets accepted with $6 service charge. $–$$*
Worth-It Rating ★★★★★

HOLIDAY INN INTERNATIONAL DRIVE RESORT This well-laid-out 13-acre resort is on the older side, with some of the problems that go with the territory. But its age also means that the landscaping is lush and mature, and it's cool and pleasant even on the hottest days. *6515 International Dr., Orlando 32819, tel. 407/351–3500, 800/465–4329 or 800/206–2747.*

654 rooms. 2 restaurants, bar, pool bar, pool, hot tub, health club. $$–$$$
Worth-It Rating ★★★★

PEABODY HOTEL ORLANDO This 27-story luxury hotel is famous as the home of the Peabody ducks. Every day, in an amazing spectacle, they take the elevator to the ground floor, and then, to the strains of John Phillip Sousa, march single file through the lobby to the fountain in the middle. Every afternoon the ceremony is reversed. The restaurants are among Orlando's best, and rooms are large, with big TV-equipped bathrooms. In west-facing rooms above the 20th floor, you can see Disney fireworks off in the distance. *9801 International Dr., Orlando 32819, tel. 407/352–4000 or 800/ PEABODY. 891 rooms, 57 suites. 3 restaurants, 2 bars, health club, hot tub, 4 lighted tennis courts, baby-sitting. $$$*
Worth-It Rating ★★★★

AT WDW: DISNEY HOTELS

DISNEY'S BOARDWALK INN Since Terrie and I spent our 18th anniversary at this faithful Disney's BoardWalk re-creation of the Atlantic City I remember from the 1950s, it's our new favorite among WDW hotels. The architecture is perfectly detailed, right down to the giant art deco signs. The hotel's Luna Park water play area features a flumelike 200-foot slide. And the fun never stops in the BoardWalk shopping, dining, and entertainment attraction at your doorstep. *WDW Central Reservations, Box 10100, Lake Buena Vista 32830, tel. 407/939–5100. 378 rooms, 14 suites. 4 restaurants, 4*

bars, health club, hot tub, fishing, 2 lighted tennis courts, baby-sitting, supervised children's program, playground. $$$
Worth-It Rating ★★★★

DISNEY'S CONTEMPORARY RESORT There's only one resort that's truly a walk away from the Magic Kingdom, and that's this five-story lakeside A-frame tower. And the monorail runs right through the middle of its giant atrium. I once stayed in the corner suite up top and had my best view ever of the Magic Kingdom's fireworks: I thought I should duck. Right on the white sand beach, there's a notable water playground-cum-pool area (one of three swimming pools) with a wading pool. *WDW Central Reservations, Box 10100, Lake Buena Vista 32830, tel. 407/824–1000. 1,053 rooms. 3 restaurants, food court, 3 bars, health club, golf, 6 lighted tennis courts, boat rental, baby-sitting, sand playground.* $$$
Worth-It Rating ★★★★

DISNEY'S DIXIE LANDINGS RESORT The world of Mark Twain's Tom Sawyer and Huck Finn was one of Walt Disney's favorite themes. With its riverboat-landing motif, this moderately priced Disney resort near Downtown Disney harks back to those days. There are six heated swimming pools; the fanciest one has slides, swings, playgrounds, and a quiet area for anyone who insists on acting like a grown-up. *WDW Central Reservations, Box 10100, Lake Buena Vista 32830, tel. 407/934–6000. 2,048 rooms. Restaurant, food court, bar, golf, bike and boat rental, playground.* $$$
Worth-It Rating ★★★★

DISNEY'S OLD KEY WEST RESORT This all-suite resort near Downtown Disney is part of the Disney Vacation Club time-share program. However, you don't have to buy in to stay

here, and the accommodations are extremely spacious and perfectly appointed, right down to the kitchens. Like many romantics, Terrie loves lighthouses. This place has several, including an impressive example that's the centerpiece of the dolphin-theme pool area, a mini-water park that's actually one of four (count 'em) swimming pools. *WDW Central Reservations, Box 10100, Lake Buena Vista 32830, tel. 407/827–7700. 497 suites. 2 restaurants, 2 bars, health club, 2 hot tubs, nearby golf, 2 lighted tennis courts, boat rental, baby-sitting, supervised children's program, playground. $$$*
Worth-It Rating ★★★★

DISNEY'S POLYNESIAN VILLAGE RESORT Imagine the huts of a Polynesian village blown up to giant size. That's the Poly, as it's known informally around here. On the monorail and on the shore of the Seven Seas Lagoon, it's also directly across the water from the Magic Kingdom, so you get a clear view of the Magic Kingdom fireworks and of the floating Electrical Water Pageant, which makes its first nightly stop here at 9 PM. The Poly is also the site of the Ohana Grill (and its fabulous island-theme show-and-feast), the wonderful Neverland Club (a kids' program), and WDW's beloved Luau—all three open to all but most convenient for hotel guests. *WDW Central Reservations, Box 10100, Lake Buena Vista 32830, tel. 407/824–3000. 853 rooms, 12 suites. 3 restaurants, bar, tiki bar, health club, golf, boat rental, baby-sitting, supervised children's program, playground. $$$*
Worth-It Rating ★★★★

DISNEY'S PORT ORLEANS RESORT The ubiquitous sound system plays New Orleans jazz in this Disney version of a Bourbon Street bivouac, near Downtown Disney. The pool, a mini-water park, has a Little Mermaid theme, and the slide

is a sea serpent named Scales; there's also a wading pool. *WDW Central Reservations, Box 10100, Lake Buena Vista 32830, tel. 407/934–5000. 1,008 rooms. Restaurant, bar, health club, hot tub, bike and boat rental, baby-sitting. $$$*
Worth-It Rating ★★★★

DISNEY'S WILDERNESS LODGE Not many Florida hotels have fireplaces. But at this upscale re-creation of a Rocky Mountain resort tucked away near Fort Wilderness there are huge stone ones in the lobby, along with some totem poles—pretty striking in this subtropical setting. Along with one basic pool, there's another replete with waterfalls and a slide down huge rocks. *WDW Central Reservations, Box 10100, Lake Buena Vista 32830, tel. 407/824–3000. 699 rooms, 29 suites. 2 restaurants, bar, golf, baby-sitting, supervised children's program. Pets accepted. $$$*
Worth-It Rating ★★★★★

DISNEY'S YACHT AND BEACH CLUB RESORTS These lakeside siblings near Epcot are almost like a single hotel, sharing amenities such as a mini water park complete with a shipwreck where your pint-sized swabs can climb up to a crow's nest, then slide down the "plank" and plunk into the not-at-all-briny deep. Both hotels look as if they had been moved straight from some vintage northeastern seaside resort. *WDW Central Reservations, Box 10100, Lake Buena Vista 32830, tel. 407/934–8000. 1,219 rooms, 71 concierge rooms, 40 suites. 2 restaurants, 4 bars, health club, golf, 2 lighted tennis courts, bike and boat rental, baby-sitting, supervised children's program, playground. $$$*
Worth-It Rating ★★★★

THE VILLAS AT THE DISNEY INSTITUTE You don't have to be attending the Disney Institute (*see* Chapter 15) to stay in these Downtown Disney–area villas, which come in several styles (all with kitchenettes). The Treehouse Villas, surrounded by woods, are a personal favorite—two-story houses with a spiral staircase between floors and one bedroom downstairs and two, with balconies, upstairs. The two-story town houses are similar in size, though more traditional. And there are five swimming pools! *WDW Central Reservations, Box 10100, Lake Buena Vista 32830, tel. 407/827–1100. 585 suites. Restaurant, bar, health club, hot tub, golf, 4 lighted tennis courts, bike and boat rental, baby-sitting, playground. $$$*
Worth-It Rating ★★★★

AT WDW IN DOWNTOWN DISNEY: NON-DISNEY HOTELS

COURTYARD BY MARRIOTT Standard rooms here are larger than any other comparable accommodations in Downtown Disney. There's a convenient deli in the lobby, and there are two swimming pools, one with a wading pool. In the restaurant, children under six eat free when accompanied by a paying adult. *1805 Hotel Plaza Blvd., Lake Buena Vista 32830, tel. 407/828–8888. 323 rooms. Restaurant, bar, health club, hot tub, playground. $$$*
Worth-It Rating ★★★★

GROSVENOR RESORT At the time of my inspection, the home of the excellent MurderWatch Mystery Theatre dinner show, was getting a much-needed refurb. The tower section has a nice view of Downtown Disney and the fireworks, and rooms have VCRs. Kids can help themselves at the kids-only buffet alongside the adult spread. And character breakfasts and dinners are held frequently on site. *1850 Hotel Plaza Blvd., Lake Buena Vista 32830, tel. 407/828–4444. 626 rooms, 7 suites. 3 restaurants, 2 bars, health club, hot tub, 2 lighted tennis courts, basketball courts, volleyball courts, shuffleboard, playground. $$$*

Worth-It Rating ★★★

THE HILTON WALT DISNEY WORLD RESORT Rooms at this former convention hotel are clean and fresh from a 1997 renovation, and each has a spacious sitting area and Sony PlayStations. There are two heated swimming pools, one with a spray-equipped wading pool. The Vacation Station kids' hotel, a hotel-within-a-hotel, was a baby-sitting adventure pioneer at WDW. *1751 Hotel Plaza Blvd., Lake Buena Vista 32830, tel. 407/827–4000. 787 rooms, 27 suites. 7 restaurants, 2 bars, pool bar, health club, hot tub, supervised children's program. $$$*

Worth-It Rating ★★★★

HOTEL ROYAL PLAZA All rooms here have balconies and VCRs, and suites have large whirlpool bathtubs. *1905 Hotel Plaza Blvd., Lake Buena Vista 32830, tel. 407/828–2828 or 800/248–7890. 372 rooms, 22 suites. Restaurant, health club, hot tub, 4 lighted tennis courts, baby-sitting. $$$*

Worth-It Rating ★★★

TRAVELODGE HOTEL For the price of a room in a Disney-owned hotel, you can rent one of the four gorgeous tropical-theme penthouse suites here. Even regular rooms are fine, and all units have a balcony, with views of Disney pyrotech-

nics from upper floors facing every direction but east. The buffet breakfast is lavish and yummy. Complimentary transportation to all parks and Pleasure Island. *1805 Hotel Plaza Blvd., Lake Buena Vista 32830, tel. 407/828–2424 or 800/348–3765. 325 rooms, 4 suites. Restaurant, café, bar, sports bar, babysitting, playground. $$$*
Worth-It Rating ★★★ Penthouse suites **★★★★★**

U.S. 192/KISSIMMEE

DAYS INN/DAYS SUITES EAST OF THE MAGIC KINGDOM Kids eat free at this motel next to the Disney's Celebration and the Old Town shopping-dining-rides attraction. Every suite has a kitchenette, and breakfast is free. *5820 W. Irlo Bronson Memorial Hwy., Kissimmee 34746, tel. 407/396–7900 or 800/327–9126. 404 rooms, 604 suites. 3 restaurants, health club, hot tub, baby-sitting, playground. Pets accepted with advance notification. $$–$$$*
Worth-It Rating ★★★

HOLIDAY INN NIKKI BIRD RESORT Rooms here are colorful and tropical. There are three heated swimming pools and two wading pools. Kids eat free. *7300 W. Irlo Bronson Memorial Hwy., Kissimmee 34746, tel. 407/396–7300 or 800/206–2747. 529 rooms. Restaurant, bar, 3 hot tubs, lighted tennis court, playground. $$–$$$*
Worth-It Rating ★★★★

HYATT ORLANDO Dominating the intersection of I–4 and U.S. 192, this rambling, well-appointed 56-acre resort is one of the most convenient in the area. There are four swimming

pools, each with its own wading pool. It's not your usual Hyatt—it's simpler, though still comfortable, more like a Hyatt motel. And without the higher Hyatt rates. *6375 W. Irlo Bronson Memorial Hwy., Kissimmee 34746, tel. 407/396–1234 or 800/233–1234. 922 rooms, 29 suites. 2 restaurants, bar, health club, 4 hot tubs, 3 lighted tennis courts, playground. $$$*
Worth-It Rating ★★★★

chapter 20
CRUISING LIKE A PRO

Back in the 1980s, the gang at Premier Cruise Lines had a neat idea: put some of the theme-park characters on a cruise ship sailing from Port Canaveral, less than an hour from Orlando, and package a short cruise with a theme-park visit and hotel accommodations. The *Big Red Boat* was such a success that it refocused cruise lines on the family market. In 1998, Disney inaugurated its own cruise line with *Disney Magic,* the first of two megaships that function as yet another Walt Disney World destination attraction. The Premiere Cruise Lines' *Big Red Boat* and ships from other lines continue to offer year-round land-sea packages from Port Canaveral with hotel accommodations and tickets for WDW and Universal Studios; you can also buy the three- or four-day cruise alone, without the land arrangements. Note: All rates given below are per person based on double occupancy.

THE DISNEY MAGIC

This Disneyesque fantasy re-creates the grandeur of the great sailing ships of the last century and the earlier part of this one. *The Disney Magic* is the only transportation to Castaway Cay, Disney's own private island destination in the Bahamas. With a land-and-sea package, you'll have a vacation that is all Disney, from the time you arrive in Orlando until you're dropped off at the airport, homeward bound. Disney Cruise Line buses transport you to a Walt Disney World resort, where you check in for your entire holiday; when it's time to head for the Disney Cruise Line's own Port Canaveral terminal, you're picked up at your hotel by another Disney bus. At the end of the trip, another Disney bus transports you back to your original hotel.

Meals and Entertainment: You'll find Broadway-style shows, first-run movies, and more dining experiences than there are meals to try them. As you work your way through a meal of California cuisine at **Animator's Palate,** the room is transformed from the first black-and-white sketch of the animator's pen into a completely animated spectacle of light and sound. **Lumière's,** named for Jerry Orbach's memorable singing candle in *Beauty and the Beast,* offers elegant five-course meals by candlelight (of course). **Parrot Cay** has a casual Caribbean theme and serves island specialties. **Palo,** a grown-up restaurant, serves Northern Italian fare with an ocean panorama. At night, the ship becomes the equivalent of a floating Pleasure Island, complete with a nighttime entertainment district, **Beat Street,** with a country-rock bar, a comedy club, a piano bar, and a sports bar. **Studio Sea,** a family entertainment area, in the form of a replica TV studio, has live bands and does game shows with audience participation.

Sports: The top deck of the *Disney Magic* is dubbed the **Wide World of Sports Deck.** Along with the more traditional shuffleboard and ping-pong, Disney has included courts for basketball, volleyball, and badminton. One deck down are the **Vista Spa** and three pools.

For Children: Kids and teens have their own activities. Grade-schoolers can join their favorite Disney characters in audience-participation skits, and Disney's **Oceaneer Club** supervises the kids and sends their parents off to play on their own. The nine-to-twelve set has its own gadget-laden adventure area, Disney's **Oceaneer Lab,** with computer stations, a giant video wall, and easy listening area. For teens, Disney offers **Common Grounds,** a coffee house with music, big-screen TV, computers, games, and a lounge. Counselors are assigned for each age group to coordinate other onboard activities for the kids. Parents are issued pagers to enable them to stay in touch with their youngsters during the cruise.

Ashore: Just when you get your sea legs, you dock in Nassau for a day, and the next day you sail to Disney's own Castaway Cay, where turquoise Caribbean waters lap at both a secluded adults-only beach and a family beach. You can get a massage, play beach volleyball, go bicycling or snorkeling, and lots more. Don't be surprised to see a dolphin.

Itineraries, Prices, Information: Cruises Fri. to Fri., with 3 days in WDW and a 4-day cruise; Mon. to Mon., with 4 days in WDW and a 3-day cruise. Rates: $1,309–$3,619, including airfare from major gateway cities (lowest late Aug.–early Dec., highest Mar.–Apr. and the year-end holidays). Disney Cruises, tel. 800/951–3532, 407/566–7000; www.disney.com/DisneyCruise.

Worth-It Rating ★★★★★

THE BIG RED BOAT

The original is still around, part of the Premier Cruise Lines fleet, and it will be for a long time. It sails the same azure ocean as Disney, but at a lower price and with a casino and duty-free shopping. And the packages include not only WDW but also my favorite, Universal Studios Escape.

You can have breakfast and photos with Looney Toons' Sylvester, Tweetie, Wile E. Coyote, Daffy Duck, Yosemite Sam, Bugs Bunny, and the Tasmanian Devil. At night you can have one of the toons tuck your kids into bed—an amazing once-in-a-lifetime tuck-in photograph!

Meals and Entertainment: As on any cruise worth its salt-water, a major objective is to feed you to death, beginning with a lavish welcome-aboard buffet. Every night brings a different theme dinner—Italian, French, American, Caribbean—with appropriate fare (or, if you must, low-fat, low-cholesterol meals that meet American Heart Association guidelines). There's even a private kids-only meal. For diversion, there are activities ranging from a family karaoke contest to a game show based on TV's old "Family Feud."

Sports: A transparent cover turns the entire Riviera deck into an indoor recreation area in inclement weather; it's the site of two large interconnecting pools and three hot tubs. There's also a fitness center with exercise equipment, and a track.

For Children: There's around-the-clock child care for youngsters two and up. There are no organized kids' programs.

Ashore: Shore excursions take you to Nassau, where you can ride in a horse-drawn carriage, take a marine-park tour, visit a casino, shop 'til you drop, and more. While Port Lucaya is not a private island like Disney's Castaway Cay, it is the next best thing, because the *Big Red Boat* is the only ship that calls here. There, as part of the Underwater Explorers Society's Dolphin Experience, you can swim with a dolphin. Sailing, windsurfing, parasailing, jet-skiing, snorkeling, scuba diving, and sport fishing are also available.

Itineraries, Prices, Information: Options include a 4-night cruise plus 3-night land package with two days at Universal Studios Escape and one-day admission to Church Street Station; or a 3-night cruise plus 4 nights' accommodations and a 4-day, 3-park Orlando FlexTicket. Both packages also include early admission to Universal Studios Escape on selected days, a Nickelodeon Kids' Park Pack, and unlimited transportation between your hotel, Universal Studios Escape, Sea World, and Wet 'n Wild. Rates: $621–$2,159 (lowest late Aug.–early Dec., highest Mar.–mid-July and during the year-end holidays). Universal City Travel, tel. 800/711–0080, 407/224–7096, fax 407/224–7001; www.destinationuniversal.com.

Worth-It Rating ★★★★

CARNIVAL CRUISE LINES

You've seen the TV ads for the world's most popular cruise line. Well, Terrie and I went on our honeymoon on the original "fun ship" (that's what Carnival calls each of its craft), the *Mardi Gras,* from Port Everglades, Miami. That was back in nineteen-eighty-something and we had the time of our lives. The *Fantasy,* the first of Carnival's new megaships, sails year-round from Port Canaveral on three- and four-day Caribbean cruises that call at Nassau and Freeport.

The ship's striking seven-deck-high atrium, with panoramic windows on the sea, computerized white minilights, and two glass elevators, is its spectacular focal point. *Meals and Entertainment:* The *Fantasy* casino is one of the largest afloat, with more than 200 slot machines and 15 blackjack tables, along with roulette, a wheel of fortune, and Caribbean stud poker. Entertainment is Vegas style—big musical productions with elaborate sets, costumes, and special effects and comedians, singers, and bands.

Terrie and I first began the trek from svelte youth to paunchy middle age on a Carnival ship, and if you take advantage of all the food put before you, you will definitely put on some pounds, although you can request vegetarian dishes or spa fare, which is low in fat, sodium, cholesterol, and calories. In the two main dining rooms, there are theme meals and one gala, usually the first night out. You can also eat on the Lido Deck at the casual, indoor-outdoor Windows on the Sea. There's also Cleopatra's, a piano bar with an ancient Egyptian theme, the Cats' Lounge, decorated with giant objects as seen from a cat's-eye view, and a disco.

Sports: The Nautica Spa offers a fine sea view as well as high-tech exercise equipment, workout areas, body and facial treatments, whirlpools, saunas, and steam rooms. There are three swimming pools, including a children's pool.

For Children: Carnival's supervised children's program, **Camp Carnival,** offers varied activities, and like Disney's, has something for each age group: 2–4, 5–8, 9–12, 13–17.

Itineraries, Prices, Information: 7-day Fantasy cruise packages include a 3-night Bahamas cruise with 4 nights' Orlando hotel accommodations and a 3-park Orlando FlexTicket; or a 4-night cruise with 3 nights in Orlando and a 3-park Orlando FlexTicket. Both packages include a tour of Kennedy Space Cen-

ter and an Alamo rental car with unlimited mileage for four days. Rates: $979–$2,389 (lowest late Aug.–early Dec., highest Mar.–mid-July and during the year-end holidays). Universal City Travel, tel. 800/711–0080, or 407/224–7096, fax 407/224–7001; www.destinationuniversal.com.

Worth-It Rating ★★★★★

index

NOTES